UNBREAKING THE *Heart*

To Robert
&
Laverne

God Bless

HOW TO FORGIVE ANYBODY FOR ANYTHING IN 5 SIMPLE STEPS

Leroy Scott MS, MDiv
Professional Christian Counselor

Request for information should be addressed to:

Leroy Scott Ministries
5635 Main Street / Ste. A / # 184
Zachary, LA 70791
leroyscott@leroyscott.com / www.leroyscott.com
(407) 622-6121

Examples cited in this book are composites of the author's actual cases. Names and facts have been changed and rearranged to maintain confidentiality.

ISBN: 978-0-578-08523-4

Scripture quotations are from the New International Version of the Bible. Copyright 2001, The Zondervan Corporation

This book is dedicated to:

My wife, Angela, and my children, Darocca, Devante and Kiswayla, for all the successes we have shared as a winning team.

The Lord is close to the broken hearted and saves those who are crushed in spirit.
~ Psalm 34:18 NIV

Contents

The Attitude Adjustment
How to Change Your Attitude
Revealing Exercises

New Memories/Better Choices
   Living Life on Purpose
   Recreating Memories
   Dreaming Again
   Going Forward: Making Healthy Choices
   Recovery Exercises

Appointment 1: On Reconciliation
Appointment 2: 43 Ways to Know You Have Forgiven

Your New Heart

A Note to the Reader

The author recognizes that readers of this book will come from different backgrounds and circumstances. Many of you will be survivors of traumatic events and this book is written for you. However, as I write, it is of course impossible for me to know whether you are a man, woman or child, or the gender of the person who was the cause of your broken heart. Nor do I know the nature or duration of the injury you suffered. It could have been the cruelest, most criminal deed imaginable; or it could have been an instance of unjust or biased treatment in the workplace. Maybe it was parental neglect. Maybe it was purely verbal abuse. It could have happened when you were a mere infant, incapable of defending yourself; or it might have occurred in adulthood, but come out of left field so you were totally unprepared for it. No one has the right to judge the depth of your hurt – a broken heart is a broken heart. We are here to mend it.

The thing is, because of these unknowns, writing about them can get a little challenging. So I have used terms like "incident," "event," "situation," "behavior" or "experience" and identifiers such as "abuser," "perpetrator" and "offender" to cover a broad spectrum of people and circumstances. You should be able to take what is written and adjust it in your mind to fit what happened in your life that broke your heart.

Of course, as stated following the title page, all names, etc., that could possibly identify actual persons have been changed and rearranged for their protection and privacy. I am eternally grateful to my clients for their candor and courage.

A word about the "assignments" in the book: at the end of each "phase" chapter, you will find several exercises where you are asked to write your responses to questions about the chapter you just read. This is *your* book, so you can of course feel free to write your answers directly on these pages. However, you could need more space for some of the exercises, so you might want to purchase a composition book – you know, like you used to use in school – so you won't feel limited in the length of your responses.

From the Author's Heart

Everyone has a past just as everyone has a purpose in life. The key to getting over an unhappy past is learning to forgive those who hurt you. You deserve to live a life free from the anxiety and pain of a time gone by. Sometimes you just have to decide that you are going to do the necessary work it takes to forgive. Holding lifelong grudges is easy, being angry for life is easy; the brave choose to do the hard work of forgiving, which leads to a life full of meaning and purpose.

This book is a gift to you and the many clients I have worked with over the past 15 years as a Professional Christian Counselor.

Thank you for allowing me into your life as your counselor to share your struggles and your successes. I know you need more than someone telling you that you must forgive. In order to fully and truly forgive, you need to understand how forgiveness works. Thanks to God and the many clients and families I have worked with in the past, you and I can now journey through the multiple facets of this principled process called forgiveness. *Unbreaking The Heart* is the spiritually practical approach to truly "letting go and letting God."

Blessings…

My love-lies-bleeding. ~ Thomas Campbell

PREFACE

The Journey of a Broken Heart

Have you ever been angry with someone because they did something to violate your trust? Maybe you were in a dating relationship or even married, and your partner cheated on you. Or maybe it was a friend or co-worker spreading rumors about you. It could even be someone who hurt you many years ago. Whatever the case, whether it was a major life-altering trauma or a minor event, it is causing life to be difficult for you. You have tried your best to hold things together, but deep down is this emotional knot reminding you there is still a wound inside that is not completely healed. You have a broken heart.

A broken heart goes through several distinct stages on its journey from pain to healing, including shock, sorrow and grief, anger, revealing (examining the facts), reconciliation and recovery. You might be at the very beginning of your journey, or you may have already gone through some of these stages and feel like you should be "over it" by now. But something is still not right with your heart.

There is a reason broken relationships hurt so much. There is a reason that broken hearts bleed so badly. Together we will journey through what happens when the heart is broken, and we will also discover ways of *unbreaking* it.

Like many people who have experienced a broken heart, you may have stopped eating and experienced difficulty sleeping. All hope for the future you once dreamed of seems lost and you may even wish you could just close your eyes and disappear from this earth. You isolated from your loved ones and closest friends. You are preoccupied with the pain of your broken heart and just can't seem to turn it around. There are even some people – eternal optimists – who have stayed in bad relationships because they are unwilling to let go of that dream they created when the relationship began; still holding onto their slim hope that things will change so their dream can come true. Is that you?

"Why did this happen to me?"

"What have I done to deserve such pain?"

"Where is God in all of this?"

"How is it that others seem so happy, but I'm having it so hard?"

Questions like these have probably been asked ever since humans became aware of their own emotions. Suffering is not fun and hard life experiences demand hard life answers. Sometimes you need someone to help you deal with the realities – straight up, with no sugar coating and no excuses. You just need to get through those difficult times, at whatever cost.

A broken heart aches to experience again the love and connection it once felt. When your heart has been broken, tears of loneliness and disappointment fall like spring rains.

Even when you stop crying on the outside, you know you're still flooded with tears on the inside. You want the pain to go away and you would do anything to have your life back again. The possibility that these feelings will last a long time seems so real to you and, regardless of what others tell you, you feel like things will never change. It seems that every day brings more moments of despair. Seconds feel like minutes and minutes feel like hours. Sunrise seems to come earlier and your waking hours seem much longer than your sleep. Facing the day is like confronting your own personal Goliath – and you forget where you left your slingshot!

Your promising future seems to have disappeared; hope has hidden itself in the darkness of despair; anger and sadness join together like perfectly matched lovers. You don't know *all* the causes of this inner turmoil, but you know it doesn't feel good. You want to escape it, but you don't know how. From the depths of your anguish, all you really ask for is someone or something to un-break your heart.

You wait and wait for relief and the longer you wait, the angrier you become. The gentleness and patience you used to have begins to turn into harshness and impulsive-ness. You want the facts in everything, and you want them quick. You don't feel like wasting time in minor things. No time for games. Laughter has run from your lips, and joy has escaped your heart.

You struggle with trying to go on with your life and wish never to return to such a place of pain. You have to work hard to ensure that no one ever hurts you again. You hear people tell you to get over it and you hear sermons on forgiving and forgetting, but no one tells you *how* to do that and somehow you know it's just not that easy.

Even when you have said you forgive verbally, there is still some deep-rooted stuff in your heart ... like a part of you that refuses to leave. You begin lying to yourself, telling yourself that you are over something that you are not over. You try to act like things are fine when you know they are not. Your heart is bleeding and the Band-Aids are not working. Sunday morning church interactions seem like a mockery as you smile and say things are great, when it truly feels like you are dying inside.

Who would have thought that a broken and bleeding heart could be so painful? Why on earth does it hurt so much? You know that God expects you to forgive, but how can you perform what you don't clearly understand? You recognize that you can't just let things go on as they are, but you need more than "just do it" as an answer to the way you feel. You need help to open and examine the secret to getting better. You need not only to say "I forgive" – you need to know *how forgiveness actually works* and where you are in the process.

In my 15 years of counseling individuals and families, I have noticed that the better a person is at forgiving others, the more complete and fulfilled they are. A person who holds grudges or doesn't effectively deal with past challenges is more likely to experience difficulties in other areas of their life. Forgiveness is, in many ways, the answer to living a truly fulfilling life.

To see life through the eyes of human vulnerability and a need for God is a necessary process for everyone. When you recognize that all humans are vulnerable to failure, rather than holding expectations of people who you yourself could not keep, you learn to live in contentment.

Unbreaking the Heart is the long-awaited Christian book on forgiveness that addresses the spiritual and emotional elements of the process. It explains in very logical ways why a broken heart hurts so much and why so many people choose *not* to get it fixed. You will learn to forgive and repair your broken heart so that you may live your life free from the bondage of unforgiveness.

FIVE SIMPLE STEPS

This book will serve as a therapeutic tool to help you get through the Five Phases of Forgiveness: Revealing, Reconciling, Redemption, Realization, and Recovery. That's it – just five simple steps. Along the way, you will gain personal insight with questions, "assignments" and journal entries.

I know personally the benefits of truly forgiving those who have hurt me and I want you to have the same experience in your life. Forgiveness is a principle you come to understand by entering into process. Forgiveness will help you get to the place *everyone* is trying to get to in their emotional life, the place you once knew so well – the place we call Love.

But how can you reach your destination if you don't know the way? You need a road map so you don't get lost on the back streets and byways, take unnecessary detours, or even make a dangerous U-turn that takes you right back where you started! And that is just what this book will give you – a clear map for your journey.

There is a reason broken relationships hurt so much. There is a reason that broken hearts bleed so badly. In this book we will examine the anatomy of a broken heart and we will also discover ways of repairing – *unbreaking* – it. Let us journey through this process together.

Had we never lov'd so kindly, Had we never lov'd so blindly, Never met – or never parted – we had never been broken-hearted. ~ Robert Burns

CHAPTER 1

THE HEART OF THE MATTER

FOUR REASONS LOVE MATTERS

In this book, you will learn that the best tool you can use to mend a broken heart is forgiveness. But, in order to understand forgiveness you have to understand how love works. At the core of forgiveness lives this fundamentally complicated principle we call love.

What really happens to love when the heart is broken and why is love so important to the life of the heart? I believe there are four reasons why love matters:

1. Love leads life.
2. Love meets needs.
3. Love is failure-proof
4. Love is the foundation of relationships.

Let's take a look at each of these reasons in detail to see why they are so important.

REASON 1: LOVE LEADS LIFE

We are born in Perfect Love and everything we do in life should be led by love. We are edified and uplifted by love. People follow love and love follows people – an endless perfect circle. But when something comes along that throws us off track and out of that perfect circle, whether it be a person who does not reflect love back to us or an indulgence we choose to entertain to our detriment or some kind of adversity we are unprepared for, then we become led by resentment, anger, fear or frustration. And where those feelings ultimately lead is to loneliness and self-pity.

There can be no sufficiency in life when love is not experienced and shared. Love is the only thing that can truly bring sufficiency to one's life. Where there is no love, there will be disharmony and division, which always leads to more pain. Division does not represent the character and nature of what God intended for humanity.

Love was not created, but always existed, just as God, Himself, has always existed. God did not step away from creation to look at love and say that it was good. Love was already there. God and Perfect Love cannot be separated – everything, including you, was shaped and framed by the character and nature of Perfect Love. You were actually created in the image and likeness of the Perfect Love that can only come from God.

God's love is the source of life. God labored for six days creating all that we see – this was the original "labor of love." That same love created both Adam and Eve. He created them from love, to love each other and to love all which He had created for them.

We begin with God in all things because we *began* with God in all things. God is so serious about love that He put it in everyone. This was God's deciding, not ours. We just reap the benefits of what it means to be created by Perfect Love – Perfect Love that would love until death to have you reign for life.

Since you began with love, you must also end with love and everything in between must be of love, because that's where you started. There is no way around it. God started something from His own nature and His own sovereign thinking. So we are what He has made us to be and we live off what He has created us from – His Perfect Love.

You were made for expressing and celebrating love. Your interactions with everything in life should reflect and represent the love God created you with. It's who you are and given to you by God, who created you. It is the lifeline to happiness and the heartbeat of contentment; without it, you will live a life of loneliness and emptiness.

There is no substitute for love. It is the source of your life and you need it to survive. You have to have it. You can't live without it. It lives and breathes who you are because God created you. He not only created you for love, but He draws you to Himself by love *(The Lord appeared to us in the past, saying: "I have loved you with an everlasting love; I have drawn you with loving-kindness." - Jeremiah 31:3)*. We can't live without it and when it stops flowing in our life, we have big problems.

If you don't have love, even your best spiritual worship is just noise *(If I speak in the tongues of men and of angels, but have no love, I am only a resounding gong or a clanging cymbal. If I have the gift of prophecy and can fathom all mysteries and all knowledge, and if I have a faith that can move mountains, but have no love, I am nothing – 1 Corinthians 13:1-2).* Imagine that – your best expression of worshiping

God is just irritating noise to His ears if love is not flowing in your heart.

This is how God clearly demonstrated Himself in Love: He sent His Son to die for us *(For God so loved the world that he gave his one and only Son, that whoever believes in him shall not perish but have eternal life – John 3:16).* Jesus died to bring people to God and to one another. The bible states that *God is love – (1John 4:8)* because only love could have done do that.

Many people make the mistake of concluding that love motivated God to give us Jesus, when, in fact, He was not motivated *by* love because He *is* love. God does not need to be motivated by anything to do something. He does what He does because of who He is, not because of how He feels. God gave His Son to the world as an expression of His character. It was an action-oriented move, rather than some feeling. Love comes from Him and is given to us as a gift. Without Him there is no possibility of even understanding love, and if we can't understand love, then we will never understand forgiveness, because the selfless act of true love is the same dynamic necessary for forgiveness.

A broken heart interferes with the natural flow of the love that God created you to experience. When we can't love, we can't truly live and where there is no love, there can be no life. When the heart breaks, love gives up. If love stops working, then life stops working. That is one of the reasons it hurts so much when you are broken-hearted. And that is why forgiveness is so necessary. The objective of forgiveness is to help love live again.

Love makes the world go 'round and when it stops living, our world stops spinning.

> Where there is no love, there can be no real life. When the heart breaks, love gives up.

REASON 2: LOVE MEETS NEEDS

Everybody needs love, whether it's a woman, a man, a five-year old child, a defiant teenager, a murderer, etc. *Everyone* is in need of love. That internal desire to be loved does not begin with you, but with God, since He created you.

Everyone wants to be connected and appreciated. Everyone wants to know that they are important, that they can make a difference and contribute to life. Everyone wants to be supported and feel like they can somehow be a part of making our word a better place. Perfect Love created everyone and everyone wants to feel perfectly surrounded by love.

But when love is not alive in you, your life may seem like it's not worth living. When love is absent, it feels like there's an empty space. Some people have literally called it a "hole in their heart."

Nothing can replace the empty space in you except God's love for you. So many people look to fill their life with pleasures and material possessions, yet the more they get, the emptier they feel. They may try alcohol, drugs, sex, money and many other things to fill this void, but nothing will suffice but God – who is love – because, you see, God created you for Himself and nothing can bring you to completeness except God.

People are complex and, because we are so complex, our needs range from the basic physiological and safety needs to the more sophisticated needs of belonging, not to mention our cognitive and aesthetic needs. Yep, that's us, need, need, need!

Some people say that the more we get, the more we need. I often wonder why these needs are so great and about the ways we try to get them met. The only conclusion I have come up with is that we were created to be interdependent – dependent on each other and on nature itself. If you think about it, we need the plants and other forms of nature to survive. Without plants, we would not have the oxygen so essential to life. Plants and animals provide the nourishment to sustain us.

But we also need the nourishment of relationships with our fellows to live fully. Regardless of how lonely and isolated a person may be, at some point they are bound to interact with someone else in some way or another. In essence we are dependent upon getting our needs met and we are wired to meet the needs of others: we are *inter*dependent.

> Love meets all needs, including the needs of others.

Samantha's Story:

Samantha was a young lady who came into counseling because she was having a difficult time in her relationship. As she discussed the problems of the relationship, she realized that some of her emotional needs she felt her husband was not meeting were the same needs her father failed to meet during her childhood. Isn't it ironic how we often invite people into our lives who are just like the person who gave us the most problems?

Samantha mentioned that her parents divorced when she was about seven years old. Like many children, she took on responsibility for the divorce, thinking that she had been so bad that it caused her parents to argue and the arguing led to the divorce. Interestingly, if you traced her thought patterns as a child, you could see how a seven-year-old could logically come to that conclusion and blame herself for her parents' decision.

Samantha recalled once getting in trouble because she didn't clean her room. Her father had just come home from a long day's work. He had been told that one of his subordinates – a less qualified person – was being promoted to a position he had applied for and he was feeling the sting of the unfairness of it.

Samantha's mom had also been stressed out because their car loan payments were more than three months behind and the creditors were threatening to come pick it up. As for Samantha, she only forgot to clean her room.

While her mother was fussing at her, Dad walked in the door. He immediately became frustrated with the tone and approached her mother to ask what was going on. He suggested that the little girl be given another chance, and he also began helping to get the room clean. This made her mother furious. She began to fuss at her husband and, when he responded, a huge argument broke out disclosing his frustration from the job and mom's frustration from the creditors. Doors slammed and voices faded into the distance. The house became silent and Samantha sat there looking around her messy room thinking, "If my room had been clean, this would have never happened."

When her parents eventually divorced, little Samantha tallied up all the times her behavior seemed to be at the center of their arguments and concluded: "If it wasn't for me, they would still be together."

Samantha needed her parents desperately, especially her father. Eventually, her mom and dad stopped talking to each other completely and her father married into another family. He lost contact with Samantha, and she became very upset. She knew her mom and dad didn't love each other anymore, but she always wondered if Dad's loss of love for Mom meant he didn't love her anymore, either. She often imagined asking him questions like, "Does not loving Mom mean you don't love me?" "Does leaving Mom mean you leave me too?"

One day Samantha wrote her father a letter explaining how she wondered if he would ever call. Or maybe he'd surprise her and come driving around the corner for a visit. Perhaps he would show up at her birthday party unannounced. After writing him the letter, she checked the mailbox every day for four weeks hoping to get a letter back from him. Unfortunately, she never received a return letter, so she also never got any answers to her questions and her problem festered inside.

Samantha was broken-hearted; she nearly lost her perspective of life completely. Wondering what would become of her broken heart, she lacked identity and often felt depressed. She felt like the weight of the world was on her shoulders.

Her father had broken her heart and now the same feelings she had as a child, she was having as an adult. It was almost like life was repeating itself all over again. Her plea for her father to be close to her was unanswered; now she continued to hope that one day her husband would be able to un-break her heart from the pain her father had made her feel. There were some things she needed from her father that she never received and because of that, she was desperately trying to find those things in her husband.

Everyone has needs that must be met in life. Regardless of how big or how small those needs are, we all have them and we all need them to be met. Through counseling, Samantha started discovering how to get her needs met appropriately in the here and now.

And what about that interdependency? There are many ways to go about meeting the needs of others, but the one thing we can be sure of is that, if we learn to *truly* love others, we will be instruments to meet their needs. Meeting the needs of the ones you love is like pointing a bow and arrow at a specific target and hitting the bull's eye every time. But you don't want to be aiming at the target with a blindfold on. You have to understand where their needs are, what they are and how you are going to meet those needs with love. You have to be the wind and strength that guide your arrow to its target. Sometimes we might have the right intentions, but we miss the mark because we had the needs wrong – we misunderstood what they were. You wouldn't want to be offering someone food when what they really need is a place to live.

True love meets needs and when *our* needs are met by love, we then are willing and able to meet the needs of others. It's the common law of love and rule of reciprocity.

REASON 3: LOVE IS FAILURE-PROOF

There are many things in life that fail, but Perfect Love is incapable of failing. After all else has failed and all methods have been exhausted, love is still going. It reminds me of the little Energizer Bunny in the commercial years ago – just keeps going, and going, and going...

Love is perfect in all its ways. It makes no mistakes and has no hidden agendas. It is also an action – it's a verb as well as a noun. Love is measured by what it does. Could you imagine if we understood God as love, but we never got to know or experience that love in action? When we don't experience principles in action, they don't mean much to us. Saying you love someone but then hurting him or her is always confusing because things must match to make sense. If you say

> There are many things in life that fail, but Perfect Love is incapable of failing.

9

you love God, it has to be reflected in your love for others.

I believe this is important because it helps us understand the long-term intention of love or, better yet, the ultimate objective of love. Love's objective is to always live and to never fail. If love could have a desire, it would desire to be alive. Not only does it not fail in all things, but true love also never decides to call it quits. So you can imagine the state of emergency you would be in if your heart was broken and in its broken condition, it attempted to make love stop working. It's like something that God created to be vibrantly live is being tempted to stop living. Now, that's an emergency if there ever was one!

In 1 Corinthians 13, the Apostle Paul writes that love is not jealous, boastful, conceited, rude, selfish or easily provoked. Nor does it continuously engage in evil or revengeful thinking. The word for "think" is an accounting term that means "keep a mathematical account." Accountants normally keep mathematical accounts of records to make sure numbers are balanced and properly budgeted. Since most of us are unable to remember all those details, we make a record of them. Love doesn't do that.

We often keep an account of the times people have withdrawn emotional, financial, and psychological energy from us. But love doesn't keep records. It simply doesn't document such things. That's because love can't hold on to things that would hinder it from continual life. So it makes sense that it would not hold grudges, keep records or even be jealous or selfish. Love's agenda is to live; but these things produce hostility and death, so if love kept such accounts, it too would die.

When we allow ourselves to keep track of such things, no matter how justified we might be, they keep us from moving on and getting through hurtful times in our own life. We get stuck.

We often want to know when we will "get over" these things, when the real question is "Can love live again?" It is more important for love to live than for you to get over something. If you think you've gotten over something, but you still feel like the love you once felt is dead, then you have probably not gotten over it at all. You are probably deeper underneath it than you realize. Maybe the burden was so heavy, you just became numb and the feelings went away, making you think you'd moved beyond the event. But in time these things have a way of resurfacing when we least expect it. That's why you have to practice forgiveness for real and on purpose and let love live again.

Sometimes life is cruel and situations are painful; it's like the love we once had is gone – or at least we are completely out of touch with it. I remember when my wife and I were dating, I had to attend military training school in another state for a few months. I will never forget how hurtful it was to leave her behind. We were young and in love. Just the thought of separating from her was painful for both of us. On the day of my departure, we parked our vehicles for a while near the interstate that would lead me to my destination, a drive of approximately 19 hours. We said our goodbyes and, as I drove that lonely highway, I cried, wondering when I would ever get the chance to see my sweetheart again. Even though I knew my training was temporary, it felt like I was leaving her for good. Boy was that scary!

And that's something like how love works. It's so much a part of us that when it feels like it's gone, we long to see it again. It's almost like it brings life. That is because it does. For me, it brought hope to realize that my darling belonged to me and I belonged to her. Every day I longed to see her again; my heart was broken in her absence. But love would not fail us. It kept us strong and kept us communicating. It kept us hopeful and imagining what the rest of our life would be like. And our unfailing love eventually brought us the gift of a life together full of affection, companionship and joy.

REASON 4: LOVE IS THE FOUNDATION OF RELATIONSHIPS

As God's love for you resides in you, it encourages and helps shape other loving relationships in your life. You are able to love because of what you have experienced in His love for you.

You were not just made for relationships; you were made for *loving* relationships. You shouldn't settle for anything else.

Because love is the essence of life and life is lived in the context of relationships, love forms the foundation of all our relationships. Love is the thing that makes relationships work. The impulse to love and be loved is the magnet that draws people together and the strength that keeps them together. Love is intentionally relational. It is designed for connection and is given to us by God out of His own loving nature.

God is relational. God created you as an opportunity to share His love for you with others. God intended for you to experience loving relationships that compliment your personality and your gifting. Truly loving relationships are healthy and well balanced; in order to have such a relationship, you must first be healthy yourself.

You must understand God's love for you, and you must also understand that He loves others through you with the same love He has for you. You have to keep that love flowing warmly in

> You were not just made for relationships; you were made for loving relationships.

your life in order to live sufficiently. When that process is broken, there is a major problem, and the diagnosis is always a broken heart. The objective is always to revive love that flows from the heart. In order to begin the process of forgiveness you must deal with the root of the issue: love.

One thing I have learned as a Christian counselor is that there isn't anything as comforting and encouraging when you are going through a difficult time as having someone with you who will listen with a compassionate ear and offer support without judgment. Psychologists and counselors normally evaluate the presence and strength of a patient's "support system," especially if sessions are expected to come to an end soon. When people are addicted to drugs or alcohol, treatment providers help them look at whom among their friends and family will support their recovery. When children and families are having difficulties at home, their support systems play a major role in the treatment prognosis. I have always said that it is better to suffer in the company of people who care about you than to suffer alone.

The age-old saying that "misery loves company" has long been interpreted to mean that negative or sad and miserable people tend to attract, connect with and be in the company of other negative people. I would like to use a different perspective. If you have ever been in a miserable state, the one thing you needed was company – a group of people who would be with you while misery took its course. Take the Bible's long-suffering Job for example: he was in an extreme state of misery and, even though his friends were self-righteous, blaming, judgmental and often wrong in their assumptions, at least he had somebody to talk to. Could you imagine 40 of the 42

> Misery not only loves company, it needs company.

chapters of the Book of Job with no conversation between Job and those around him? Now, that would be a sad story. He was in the worst state imaginable, with God sending all sorts of afflictions to test his faith. Fortunately, people came to talk to him, even if they did not agree with him.

Misery not only loves company, it needs company. When a person is miserable or feeling down, they will normally need someone else to lean on for support. The point is that people need people. People need interactions that bring out the best in them during the worst moments of life.

When you ask yourself what drives this phenomenon of the need for other people in your life, the answer is quite clear. Throughout this book, we stress that God is love and He created you for love. The battery that drives the need for connection is love. Love is what relationships are built on. Longing for love is what causes us to seek out relationships. Without love there would be no need for relationships because there would be no drive for such connections.

Could you imagine life without loving relationships? I mean, mothers would not love their newborn babies and fathers would not feel love towards their sons and daughters, so the instinct to nurture would be missing and families would not flourish. A daughter whose mother was dying would not be able to grieve that loss. A young man and young women would not feel the strong pull of love. Life would be sterile and empty; without love, relationships would be something yet to be discovered.

But thankfully that is not the way life is. We are full of love and live by love. We actually live to love and we love learning how to be in love. My first book, *Creating Possibilities in Marriage*, was a workbook that helped couples communicate and deepen their love for one another. As I spoke across the country and did workshops from the book, I learned that people in general are very interested in learning how to be in love. They feel there is something about love that will make their life work well. It is almost as if the better you get at it, the better life is for you. That's when I began thinking about the "broken heart." If love is so natural for us, I thought, then to not have it must be extremely detrimental and counter to our created design. I began exploring what things help to strengthen our understanding of our need to be loved and also to be in love.

Just as certain vegetables or vitamins are good for you because they promote healthy blood flow, I found the same is true with love. So I made a list of things that should be in your love diet.

I can hear you now: "Oh no, not another diet!"

One of the hardest things for most people is to change their diet or unhealthy eating and drinking habits. Drastic changes often come when the person is diagnosed with a fatal illness. But even then, it is sometimes very difficult to change. Well, here is a list of things that will help to encourage and strengthen your Love Life. This is your to-do list of things to add to your heart-healthy diet. It might seem hard at first but, like any habit, it gets easier if you stick with it.

1. Trust

First and foremost, you should add trust to your love diet. Trust is a main ingredient of a healthy love life. Trust means to have confidence or faith in someone or something without being afraid or anxious the outcome. It is rooted in the certainty that everything will work out in your favor.

Trust is not a trait we are born with; rather, it is developed over time.

Unlike love, trust *does* keep a record of its outcomes. Trust increases and decreases based on its experience. It is a trait of believing in the reliability of others. Its objective is to have complete confidence in a person or thing. When it is broken, it hides itself in a corner, peeking out every now and then to see if it is safe to come out again.

If trust is broken in one area of life, it becomes afraid to operate in other areas of life as well. Because of the frailty of people, you have to help trust to understand that people fail and not all people will meet expectations. You have to coach trust into the championship game, helping it to operate with balance. Because the game of life is a hard one to win, the more you balance your trust, the better your relationships will be.

Don't rush trust, but let it develop over time. It wants to be a part of you as much as you want to be a part of it. It is lonely not to have it, and it is foolish to have too much trust in a person or thing. To trust God is wise and to have people and friends you can trust is grace. Try adding trust to your love diet, but do it in small portions in areas you feel safe and where there is a record that will validate its existence.

2. Communication

Communication conveys information. Without information there would be no way for people to operate together. Communication is most necessary when two people have to accomplish a task together. That's why when communication breaks

> There is no success where there isn't effective communication going on.

down, it can be catastrophic. If it happens in crisis, people die; if it happens in war, the battle is lost; if it happens in a game, the game is lost, and if it happens in a marriage, the marriage fails. There is no success where there isn't effective communication going on. In technology, if one system cannot communicate with another, both systems will fail. Even in your body, if your eye says to your hand, "I don't need you," the eye becomes useless. We are not only interdependent on one another, we must communicate in order to function at full capacity.

Communication is married to love because, without communication, you can't have a loving relationship. That's like having God without His word. So, add communication to your love diet. And yes, I understand some people are hard to talk to and many people will not understand you, but you still have to be talking if you want something to work well. You have to make the effort. Take the risk and begin conversations in public. Stop passing people by without saying "hello." Let people know who you are and what you do. Tell your family good evening and good night, even if you have to do it like the Waltons – "Good night, John Boy." Talk, talk, talk – the health of your heart depends on it!

3. Connection

Connection means to be associated with others in a relationship that brings ideals, events, memories and imagination together. Think about it; being connected is such a human phenomenon and so much a part of you, it's scary to think of life without it. Everyone wants and is wired for connection. The better you are at getting into circles that help to drive your ideals and dreams, the better your life will be.

When your heart has been broken, your love wires disconnect themselves. Find a way to reconnect them because, if you don't, you'll be left disconnected in many other areas of life. One of the most miserable experiences in life is when you are always around people who don't make you feel like your imaginings and goals – your future visioning – have value.

Your life is as good as the people you live it with, so make it a priority to get connected to good people and be sure loneliness is not an option. There is no better way to make a strong connection than looking into the sky with a person you love and dreaming together.

> Your life is as good as the people you live it with ...

4. Hope

The value of living in a hopeful frame of mind is greatly underestimated in life. The whole concept of *Unbreaking the Heart* is based on having hope restored to your life. We will be talking a lot about hope later in the book, so I will limit this section to a discussion about why you should have it added to your love diet.

Hope is not just a feeling or desire that something will happen; it is the outward expression of faith *(Now faith is being sure of what we hope for and certain of what we do not see – Hebrews 11:1)*. Faith is a component of hope, but it's hope that you see operating. In church, we talk a lot about faith, and justifiably so because we are saved by grace through faith. Still, I think we would benefit from discussing hope more often.

Hope is the face at the front of all things desired or believed. Hope fights from the front line of the battle. It clears the way for the rest of your mind to dream about making something happen. To hope is to set yourself apart from your experiences and your abilities. Hope is radically positioned to grasp the impossible and to receive the invisible. To say that you are hopeful about something breaks through the sometimes negative elements of human life with a belief in an end that might be difficult to envision at first. You don't have to be a Christian to have hope. That's why you will find people of all faiths, or none, who are hopeful and accomplish what they desire. Yet there are many people who have faith in God, but lack hope. When their heart was broken, their faith in God remained, but their hope was impacted. So faith in God does not always equal hope in life, especially when the heart is broken.

Faith and hope have to cut though doubt like a double-edged sword, and you have to swing from both sides. Adding hope to your life will bring a smile to your face. Be hopeful for small things and then celebrate your hope and appreciate your moments of being able to experience it.

Always have something to hope for. Most people talk about what they are thankful for. Gratitude is wonderful, but these concern things that have already happened. You need to hope for things that haven't occurred yet. You should always have things that haven't happened on your list, so that hope can always live in you. Just a teaspoon of hope a day is better than nothing.

When any of these four (trust, communication, connection, hope) is violated or neglected, it affects the natural flow of love. When these break, the heart breaks; then love begins to suffer and die out in your life. When the heart is broken, love begins to give up and that is so counter to what you were created for, that your body goes into survival mode and everything in you goes haywire just trying to protect you from the pain of that broken heart. So be sure to keep hope high on your heart-healthy menu!

Love deserves to be respected. That is why you should always treat love as though it could leave you. When love is absent from your life, you may think you are fine, but in reality you are not. You yearn for the day when you see yourself loving and being loved again. I don't mean you have to be in a relationship. What I am saying is that there is a unique relationship we all share with love because it is so much a part of us; and when it's not there, we miss it and long to see it again. Having a broken heart is the body's way of expressing the emotional hurt you experience when someone has harmed you. That's why we have to keep on loving people even when it hurts and let love work its wonders.

Therefore, the greatest gift you can give yourself is helping love live in your life. There is really no substitute for love. When all is said and done, it is at the heart of the matter.

Hearts will never be made practical until they are made unbreakable. ~ The Tin Man (Wizard of Oz)

CHAPTER 2

ANATOMY OF A HEALTHY HEART

THE 4 CHAMBERS OF YOUR EMOTIONAL HEART

The heart pumps blood to every organ in your body. It is said to be one of the strongest muscles in the body. Regardless of whether its beats are consistent or irregular, it out-works other muscles by far. It is always in the weight room working out. Even while you are in your deepest sleep, it's working.

Your heart is always thinking of you and working to keep you alive, whether you appreciate it or not. It has a job to do and it's serious about getting it done.

But, the heart is more than just a muscle that pumps blood through your body. The Bible considers it the seedbed of all human emotions *(Above all else, guard your heart, for it is the wellspring of life – Proverbs 4:23)*, meaning that not only does it keep you alive physically, but also it carries the joy of love, beauty, fulfillment of desires *and* the

> The Bible considers the heart to be the seedbed of all human emotions.

weight of all stress, anxiety, anger and other feelings. The Bible says that out of the heart flow all the issues of life.

To help us understand what makes a healthy emotional heart, picture it – like your physical heart – as having four chambers. Each chamber has a particular function and each is also dependent upon the others to work effectively. As you can see in the graphic below, love moves through the heart, and in a healthy heart, this flow is effortless.

The four chambers are (1) the Confession Chamber, (2) the Reactive Chamber, (3) the Attitude Chamber and (4) the Life Filtering Chamber. Each chamber helps you respond emotionally and intellectually to your experiences and to establish a healthy life perspective around those experiences.

THE EMOTIONAL HEART

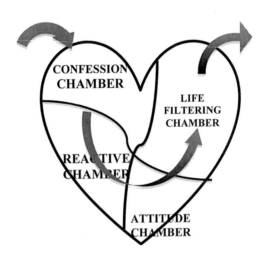

CONFESSION CHAMBER

The Confession Chamber knows the facts and recognizes all the details. It is totally impartial and tells the truth about any situation. The Confession Chamber is that part of the heart that is purely honest about the experience. It knows how you feel about things, but it doesn't play games with the way something has made you feel and just simply tells it like it is.

 ## REACTION CHAMBER

The Reaction Chamber, unlike the Confession Chamber, asks the question, "How do I feel about this?" It is the part of the heart that takes the facts from the Confession Chamber, analyzes them and then makes the *Feeling Decision*. It knows you well enough to make an informed decision about how you are supposed to feel about what has happened. It understands when you say "My heart just can't take anymore!"

 ## ATTITUDE CHAMBER

Facts and feelings are not the end of the process. The Attitude Chamber decides how to join these facts and feelings together. It looks at the facts in the Confession Chamber and the feelings in the Reaction Chamber, and decides how you will *think* about the incident now and in the future – what your opinion of it should be.

 ## LIFE-FILTERING CHAMBER

Just as blood has to exit the heart, so does the incident. It exits the heart through the Life-Filtering Chamber. This part of the heart determines how you will behave and interact with the outside world as a result of what has happened. It filters the details of the event, the feeling produced by the event and the thinking created by the event and, in doing so, it gives life to either hope or despair. If filtered by hope, it gives you the opportunity to see the truth of your ability to survive the event. If filtered by despair it discourages you from progressing and working through this great pain.

- **Confession Chamber** – Holds the details and truth of life experiences.

- **Reactive Chamber** – Represents feelings you experienced as a result of a particular event.

- **Attitude Chamber** – Represents the collection of thoughts, feelings and actions produced by a particular event.

- **Life-Filtering Chamber** – Represents how events are finally filtered (either with hope or despair). It is the final chamber, and it determines your actions in the future, relative to the events in your life.

My love lies bleeding. ~ *Thomas Campbell*

CHAPTER 3

WHEN LOVE IS DYING

AN EMOTIONAL PERSPECTIVE

There is a condition known as "Broken Heart Syndrome," a term coined by Japanese doctors. They found that the heart of a person who has suffered a stressful or traumatic event is affected physically. Part of the person's heart is enlarged and other medical problems become evident, similar to a heart attack. The condition is treated medically and patients are normally hospitalized for up to a week.

The heart is a massive tool designed by God to promote the function of life. It is strategically protected by a set of bones to ensure its safety. It keeps life-blood flowing through your body. If it is harmed in any way or if it stops beating, it can't pump blood through your body and where there is no blood, there is no life *(...because the life of every creature is its blood... – Leviticus 17:14)*. So, if the heart is not working properly, you can't experience life to its fullest. The paradox is that when the emotional life of the heart is injured, one can be physically alive, but personally empty and emotionally dead.

Many people who have experienced a heart attack say that it feels like a heavy weight pushing down on their chest. A client told me once that it felt like an elephant was sitting on his ribcage. You may have seen movies – or maybe you have even experienced this in real life – where someone has a heart attack and the EMTs rush in and begin trying to revive the heart. Their ultimate objective is to make it beat again. They push on the chest, blow air in the lungs and sometimes shock the body to stimulate the heart. They do whatever it takes, because if the heart is not fixed, life, which is in the blood, can't reach the rest of the body. The objective is to fix the heart and fix it quickly. In repairing the physical heart, we restore physical life. In repairing the emotionally broken heart, we restore emotional and spiritual life.

A broken heart can feel just as uncomfortable as a heart attack. It makes you feel like there is no tomorrow. It can trigger feelings of hatred, frustration, anger and depression. You may experience feelings that make you want revenge on the person who broke your heart, or you may begin taking your anger out on yourself. A broken heart can leave you saddened and lonely with only time and questions on your hands. What do you do when the heart is broken? What happens when love decides to quit? Where do you go for help?

Whenever love stops in a relationship, the relationship becomes unhealthy. A client of mine mentioned that her husband told her that he loved her, but he was not in love with her, as though simply being with her was enough. There is a subtle difference between loving someone and being "in love" with them.[1] But, most people don't make that distinction correctly and I think when someone says this to you, what they are really trying to say is that they don't want to be with you anymore. It would help if they

---

[1] This is explained at length in Note 14 of my book, *Love Notes* (see Other Products at the end of this book).

could just be honest and say that, rather than letting you hang on to the hope that they will continue to love you and be with you. Being honest could help to prevent many broken hearts.

I have heard both adolescents and adults who were incarcerated claim that they love their mother, but in many cases they were the ones causing their mothers great pain through their actions. I cannot count the number of times I have seen mothers and grandmothers hanging onto jail cells bars, pleading with law officials to give their sons a break, only to be faced with disrespect and unfaithfulness from the same sons they are trying to help.

These young men put more energy into listening to the so-called "friends" who got them in trouble than listening to their own mothers who were always there for them. Getting them to understand that you don't hurt the ones you truly love is always challenging. "Instead," I tell them, "you would stop your mother's tears by not doing wrong – or prevent them by not straying into wrongdoing in the first place.

"Sometimes it's not until you lose someone you really love that you truly begin to appreciate them," I warn. "And sometimes the people you love depart this life unexpectedly and leave you with a broken heart. That is why it is better to appreciate every day you're given to be with the ones you love."

Anyone who has been in love knows that, when you lose someone you love, it hurts to the core of your being. Love causes you to beg a person to come back; it tells you that person is the source of its (love's) life. Love will always stretch itself towards that person even when it lands in empty places. It would rather reach and miss than give into the fact that things are no longer the way they used to be.

Love never really anticipates the loss. It assumes that life will always be the same. That's why it's easy to take the people who are most supportive of us for granted – believing they will always be there for us – and instead put our energy into the people who are not always there for us or create problems in our lives.

Love must be the response to loss. Sometimes in life the past doesn't equate to the present, and the future begs for clarity. Since love is at the core of human life, then the future of life's greatest fulfillment always has love in its equation. You have to learn to love even when it is difficult.

Carmen's Story:

I remember when Carmen came into my office and said that her high school boyfriend had broken her heart. Her parents had actually referred her for counseling because she had recently become pregnant by this boyfriend. She had been dating him for about three years and had trusted him with so much of herself. But when he heard that she was pregnant, he was not mature enough to accept his responsibility and left her high and dry. She felt abandoned because she never dreamed this would happen. She had told him her secrets, talked about her parents, dreamed of her future, and placed her heart in his hands. There was no real reason for her to believe that they would not grow together. She had felt that beside each other they would conquer the world. They made promises to one another. They laughed and cried together. "We just seemed so inseparable," she said during one of her sessions.

As she continued telling her story, Carmen interrupted herself frequently to be sure I understood how real their love for one another was. She finally said, "You think it's puppy love or infatuation?" She was surprised when I said, "No. I think you were in love, and I think your love for him was just as real as you thought it was. It was your love. It belonged to you and you gave it away. That's as real as it gets."

You see, you have to be honest with yourself. Just because you are mad and broken-hearted now, doesn't mean that your previous love and relationship with a person were not real. You probably had some very enjoyable experiences with the person who broke your heart and those experiences don't need to be minimized. Good people can do bad things, just as bad people can do good things. Just because it ended the way it did, doesn't mean you have to throw all of the experience and time away.

Carmen later began to identify with her pain. She felt very guilty because she believed she had sinned against God. She frequently stated that she knew God was not pleased with her because she had engaged in a sexual relationship before marriage. She consistently cried, "I'm sorry, I'm sorry," but her feelings of guilt would not alleviate the pain that anger was causing her. She knew something was missing, and she began to say so.

"I feel like a big part of me has been ripped away. I will never forgive him for just leaving me like this." She began to talk as though her boyfriend was sitting right next to her. She was angry and wanted him to know it.

The interesting thing was that, unless Carmen worked through this great loss, she would forever seek someone outside herself to alleviate the pain of this experience. Unless she learned to forgive her boyfriend, her life would forever be controlled by feelings of rejection and abandonment. She might even project those feelings on her child, if she wasn't careful.

Carmen's heart was broken and love was giving up fast. She needed some help and now she was going to get it.

She was both tired of her guilt and anger, and motivated to change, and that was enough to convince her that she could get through this difficult time.

THE ANATOMY OF A BROKEN HEART

To give relevance to the statement "My heart has been broken," we will again use the heart as a model. There may be no medical or scientific significance to this emotional analogy of the heart, but I believe it will help you put your feelings and forgiveness in perspective.

Following the initial thought that we were created by love and for love and that love flows to us by God and through us to others, we will consider the heart as the place where all human emotions reside. The objective is to help you consider that, when love stops flowing through you, it is simply the result of a broken heart, which leads to a difficult and painful reality.

THE STAGES OF A BROKEN HEART:

1. Shock – A blow to the heart.
2. Sorrow/Grief – How could they?
3. Anger – That rat!
4. Revelation – Looking at the facts without judgment.
5. Recovery/Healing – Where do I go from here?
6. Reconciliation– I'm o.k. and so are you.

Karen and John's Story:

Let me tell you the story of Karen and John, and how Karen moved through some of these stages. As a young couple, they seemed inseparable. They met as teenagers and married during their young adult years. Karen felt John was the best thing that ever happened to her. They grew together, dreamed together and shared all the aspirations of their young adult lives. Nearly two years after being married, God blessed them with their first child, who John proudly named Kathy after his mother. Kathy was the prize of the family and John knew that this was his opportunity to become the father he had dreamed of being.

Karen was always proud of the way she felt about Kathy's father. Not only was he a great husband, but he was also a very good dad. He spent countless hours entertaining Kathy with games, movies and other activities. Watching John as he interacted with Kathy, Karen felt somewhere deep inside she also was experiencing the father's love she had never known. John was always available to his wife and always made sure his family was provided for. For these two ladies, he was a hero.

One morning when Kathy was about five years old, she kissed her father, John, goodbye as he walked out of the door to go to work. She walked behind him to his motorcycle and waved to him as he drove off. Her mother watched behind as little Kathy blew kisses to her father. Kathy kept her eyes glued to him until she couldn't see him anymore. Once he had traveled beyond her sight, she playfully turned towards her mother and walked back into the house.

STAGE 1: Shock

Later that afternoon, the phone rang. Anticipating an ordinary call, Karen said, "hello." There was silence on the other end for a brief moment. Then a very serious voice began to utter words that would turn Karen and Kathy's life upside down.

"This is Bob with the local police department," the man said. "Bob," Karen said. She knew her husband would never do anything to be put in jail, so jumped to the conclusion that it was some Police Association raising money. "I'm not really interested at this time sir. Try us some other time."

"No," said the officer. "I have some bad news for you." "Some *what?*" asked Karen. He replied, "I'm sorry to tell you this, but your husband was involved in an accident, and the rescue workers were unable to save him."

Karen was speechless.

"You mean he's dead?" she asked.

"Ma'am, I'm sorry," said the officer.

STAGE 2: Grief/Sorrow

Karen dropped the phone. But within just a few minutes, she was able recover enough to disassociate from her own pain as she pictured her daughter waiting for her dad to come roaring down the street on his motorcycle. It was like being hit in the chest twice with a ton of bricks. The first shocker was her own grief. The second was the grief she felt for her daughter.

Karen did not tell Kathy immediately. She actually tried to get Kathy to play in the back yard that evening so that she wouldn't be waiting by the front door to see her father coming down the street. But as they were in the back yard, Kathy's intuition told her that it was almost time for daddy to come home. She bolted to the front door and waited as she usually did. Karen ran to the bathroom to cry in secret.

Five o'clock passed and Kathy asked, "Where is dad?" Six, seven and eight o'clock passed and still no daddy. Karen was not strong enough just yet to let Kathy know that her father was killed in an accident. At about 8:30 that evening the sound of a motorcycle caused Kathy to run to the front door, but it wasn't her father. Kathy eventually fell asleep in her mother's arms as her mother rocked her in her dad's recliner.

Karen could not sleep that night. At times she felt like she could hardly breathe. All she had to hold on to was a daughter who was still waiting for her daddy to come home. Love was reaching for something that was now gone and, boy, was it hurting! Karen rocked and rocked while Kathy waited and waited and still no daddy.

As the days went by, Karen explained to Kathy that her father had been in an accident. At the same time, Karen realized that she was beginning to feel the stirrings of anger in her broken heart because she felt like John had abandoned his family. Of course, she knew that wasn't really the case, so she recognized that something was wrong in her heart. Her love turned to sorrow and her sorrow was just beginning to meet with anger. Karen began to realize that when the heart breaks, love begins to stop and when love stops everything goes haywire.

STAGE 3: Anger

If you have ever had your heart broken, you probably remember how anger and hatred began, like a systemic poison, to creep into your very being. The reason you hurt so much is because you once trusted and/or loved that person. Your expectations of the person were higher than the fault they committed. You gave them a chance, and they hurt you. When you hoped that they would do well by you, they did just the opposite. For example, in the case of an abusive situation, the victim hopes to have a good loving and dependable relationship, but when it turns abusive, this hope fails and love is lost.

Love is not just love for a person, but also the passion you feel for your plans and dreams for that particular relationship – the ideal future you form in your mind's eye for what could be between you and that person, whether a lover, a parent, a friend or even a boss or co-worker.

If, as you grew up, you found yourself beginning to hate your mother or father, it's because as a child you rightfully expected to have a good, loving relationship with them. You assumed your parents had unconditional love for you. When you realized you weren't getting that, hope failed and love was lost.

If you have been in a romantic relationship (or at least that's what you *thought* it was) and your partner cheated on you, you become upset because you hoped for a relationship that was honest and truthful. When your partner cheats, love is lost and hope fails. Hope *always* fails when love is lost.

> Hope always fails when love is lost

If someone on your job does you wrong, you become resentful because you want that person to notice your hard work and respect your efforts and dedication to the job. When they don't, you feel disrespected and love is lost.

The only reason a broken heart hurts so much is because you once trusted and/or loved the person who broke it. You hoped for something that did not happen the way you planned and, since the plan didn't work, hope failed and love was lost – leaving the heart broken and turning your life upside-down.

Seeking revenge is a natural response to being hurt. For some reason when love is tampered with or rejected, we often feel a need to retaliate, and we can do so with extreme revenge: holding grudges, hating, resenting, and hoping to see the one who hurt us also suffer pain in their life. Even if we say we are not upset, somewhere deep inside, we want revenge. You may think you don't want to be angry, but it's as if your body refuses to listen to your rational mind and just gets angry on its own. That's because this is how your body protects itself from danger.

Have you ever thought about what happens when you cut yourself? White blood cells are automatically released and rush to the cut to begin the body's natural healing process. That's the same way we react to someone hurting us emotionally. We feel attacked and automatically respond in defense; we prepare ourselves for revenge. If we don't react physically, then all of those emotions are stored up in our heart and we grow bitter, cold and often times resentful and hard to get along with.

Our human nature is to take revenge on the one who hurt us. If this were not human nature, there would have been no reason for God to remind us in the Scriptures that vengeance belongs to Him *(Do not take revenge, my friends, but leave room for God's wrath, for it is written: "It is mine to avenge; I will repay," says the Lord – Romans 12:19).* In other 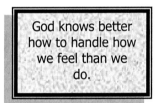 words, God is telling us to relax, and He will handle in His own way what you are feeling inside. The feeling is acknowledged, but the response is up to God, and He knows better how to handle our emotions than we do. In many ways, we are limited in our ability to know what to do regarding how we feel.

But why is it so painful and why do you feel so much aggressive passion? It's almost the opposite extreme of what you once felt for that person. Your loving passion has

God knows better how to handle how we feel than we do.

turned inside out and now you passionately hate the very same person.

As the grief process began to set in for Karen, she came into counseling to get help navigating through the different stages of grief and to find emotional support in her difficult time. Following his death, Karen learned that her husband had incurred a tremendous amount of debt that she was unaware of. Among several other issues related to grief and loss, this young widow would have to deal with how she was going to forgive her husband for leaving her with so many secret financial burdens. In addition to her growing anger about those things, she began to feel resentment towards John about the things they dreamed of together that would now never be realized. They would never build the house they wanted together. They would never cruise the oceans as they had envisioned.

Real love is rooted in the heart. It flows fluidly and reaches out to the people you truly care about. And when someone is no longer there, its reach lands in an empty space. Karen's love was still reaching out, but now it had nowhere to land and anger was beginning to choke the love out of her life.

(Discussion of the stages of a broken heart continues in Chapter 4: 911 – Forgiveness to the Rescue.)

REPAIRING THE HEART

Some of the procedures performed during heart surgery include cutting, patching, changing and stitching back up. Some operations are more complicated than others and require more intense procedures. The same is true for the emotionally broken heart; sometimes it will require just a little personal evaluation and a few changes, while other times it may take a lot more than that.

Okay, let's play a little here with the metaphor of open-heart surgery to lead us through the steps of repairing a broken heart. Each of the members of the medical team – doctors, nurses and staff – has a role to perform and goes through specific procedures from diagnosis to aftercare. We're going to see how healing a broken heart follows similar stages.

Forgiveness is the scalpel we'll use to cut out anger, fear and resentment. Then we're going to stitch you back up and keep close watch over you in the recovery room so your heart can truly heal.

Like the human heart, the emotional heart has many parts. Each part has a particular function. Each part is also dependent upon the other parts in order to work effectively. When one part is damaged the whole heart is broken. The objective is to identify what part is affected and begin working through it to restore the heart to normal functioning. As you saw in the previous chapter, love moves through a healthy heart, but a broken heart prevents the constant and smooth flow of love and it gets blocked somewhere in the process. As a result, you become broken-hearted and your love begins to lose its life. Remember that love was designed to be failure-proof but with a broken heart its life begins to suffocate and is in desperate need of resuscitation.

> **A WORD TO THE WISE:**
> If your broken heart is affecting your day-to-day ability to effectively perform daily tasks, or you have become overwhelmed with the pain associated with your broken heart, that may be beyond the scope of this book to help you and you should consider seeing a professional counselor.

CHAPTER 4

911: FORGIVENESS TO THE RESCUE

FORGIVENESS SAVES LIVES

When the pain of a broken heart is new, it seems unbearable. But as much as it feels like it, understand that *you* are not dying, but it is love that is letting go of its hold on life. You can't give up in the middle of the pain; you have to go through it and keep love alive. Even though a broken heart weakens it, love must be revived.

So here you are in the Emergency Room of Life! You've been given the diagnosis: a badly broken heart. Now what?

Now – *forgiveness!!*

Forgiveness is the resolution of anger and restoration of hope. It is the tool that will allow your love to live again. This does not mean the situation that broke your heart will change, but the spirit of forgiveness – the compassionate feeling that indicates you are willing to let go of anger, hurt and blame – will cause your heart to reverse its direction so you can live a life beyond that pain in the happy self-determination for which Christ has set you free. Once you realize that, you will be better able to navigate through the pain of a broken heart.

Forgiveness is a life-time plan with five phases (the five steps of our title). We'll describe those shortly, but you can't even get started through the phases until you first *make the **choice** to forgive.*

Like most things in life, forgiveness is something that you have to choose. A surgeon requires the patient to sign a consent form giving them permission to do surgery. Well, the Great Physician needs you to make a choice as well. This may be emergency surgery, but it is also *elective surgery!* It is the choice that gets you into the operating room.

In principle, God commands forgiveness, but the choice to forgive is a very personal one. No matter how much you say you trust God or how much faith you have, it takes a lot to turn the other cheek *("You have heard that it was said, 'Eye for eye, and tooth for tooth.*[39] *But I tell you, Do not resist an evil person. If someone strikes you on the right cheek, turn to him the other also." – Matthew 5:38-39).* God instructs you not to seek personal revenge on your offender, but to demonstrate love and accountability toward that person, holding them responsible for what they did while simultaneously loving who they are (more on that later).

Forgiveness has many roads that all lead to one destination. For some people forgiveness is expected: the principles of their life force them to do it. This is the case for most Christians. For others, it can be done as a trade. As long as what they lost is returned, then they will forgive. If what they lost is not restored, then they will not forgive. Some people even use forgiveness as a way to get back at a person. They will forgive someone and then hold it over their head for the rest of their lives. All too often, I have seen people in relationships use this "holier-than-thou" attitude as a weapon. They forgive their partner for doing wrong, but never let them forget it, reminding them that being forgiven is a privilege they did not deserve. Or they may forgive as long as things are even – the "you cheated, so I cheated; now we're even so let's start over" attitude. Forgiveness can also be used to keep peace. To avoid conflict, some people just let things pass.

Then there is forgiveness as an act of love. This type of forgiveness does not seek to control another person, is not revengeful and always creates an opportunity for reconciliation. This kind of forgiveness goes way beyond feeling sorry. When feeling sorry is not enough, forgiveness answers the cry for hope.

So, now it's your decision. What will you choose to do and why will you choose to do it? You can choose to hold on to the things that hurt you and bottle up feelings of resentment and hostility towards another person, or you can choose forgiveness. You can act like things that are hurting you are not bothering you – causing extreme emotional pressure on yourself – or you can choose forgiveness.

You might feel a need to hold on to it (the resentment, hurt or anger) for a while because you are not ready to let it go. But what you are not understanding is that a decision to forgive is not a cure in and of itself. A statement of forgiveness is only a *representation* of your willingness to endure the consequences of the decision. Forgiveness is not easy and it literally requires dependence on God to sustain you as you go through the stages of the process.

It's your heart that has been broken. It's your love that has stopped living. And it's your choice to get it fixed.

You are now the EMT. You are both the patient and the doctor. It's up to you to get it done and it is also up to you to do it. If ever God gave you responsibility for anything, He has truly given you responsibility now. You can choose to allow love to live or die.

Denis Waitley once said that *there are two primary choices in life; to accept conditions as they exist, or accept the responsibility for changing them.* Regardless of how the heart was broken, it must be repaired. You have to decide that you are tired of living in unforgiveness. It may have been your father, mother, family member, best friend, husband, wife or any other person who caused the hurt. The choice is yours and no one can make it for you. You have the instructions and you understand the seriousness of the situation. It's your choice now. The ball is in your court. What will you choose?

Make that choice now and seal it by checking one of the two statements below:

_____ I choose forgiveness. I choose to let love live in me and through me.

> Pray this prayer: *Thank you Lord for Your divine presence in my life. Thank you for forgiving me of my sins and restoring hope to my life. I have been hurt badly, and I am desperately trying to figure it all out. I have noticed that anger has grown in me and thoughts of revenge have surfaced. Unlike You Lord, I am having a hard time forgiving what happened. I am so in need of Your help, Lord. I commit this process to You, and I commit my heart to You and ask that You free me from the need for self-control and grant me complete dependence on You. If I accept the things that have happened, then I must also accept the fact that You allowed them. Pardon my emotional struggles to understand, and give*

*me patience to realize Your greatness in it all.
I am a sinner, hurt and broken for You. No
better or worse than my offender. We need
Your help and I'm open to doing for them
what You have done for me. Help me.*

_____ I decline forgiveness and don't care whether love lives or dies.

> You absolutely have the right to choose this
> option. However, before you decline
> forgiveness, you may want to read the rest of
> this book because it can help you understand
> why you feel the way you do concerning your
> offender and your situation. Forgiving
> someone has great implications. Some of
> those implications may mean giving up the
> anger that has now become a motivator for
> your life – what I call the "I'm going to show
> them that I can make it" syndrome.

At this point, forgiving may be the farthest thing from your mind and even entertaining the thought that this person can get away with what they did to break your heart seems absurd. But sometimes you have to try things on the outside to realize them on the inside.

In most cases you can live your life from the inside out, but here is one of those circumstances when you just have to do it and wait for the feeling to follow. This one is done from the outside – in.

If your feelings are too afraid to go first, you might have to let your rational mind lead you in this instance and then convince your feelings that it's safe to come along, too. Take the action and let the feelings follow.

In Deon's story, below, we continue the examples of the stages of a broken heart while furthering the discussion of how forgiveness does its healing work.

STAGE 4: Revealing the facts

<u>Deon's Story</u>

I remember when my client Deon realized that one of the reasons he had not forgiven his father for leaving the family was because he *needed* to be angry with his father in order to be motivated to do better for his own family than his father had done for him. After nine years of college and the birth of his first child, Deon came into therapy saying he needed help forgiving his father for not being there for him. After several sessions, the fellow eventually made a list of the benefits of being angry with his father. His list looked a little like this:

"Being angry with my father…

1. Motivated me to be a good person;

2. Motivated me to finish college;

3. Motivated me to work hard and get a good job;

4. Motivated me to be a good husband;

5. Motivated me to be successful."

I pointed out the paradox: "Wow, you must really love the man you hate so much to live your entire young life proving to him that you could be better than him!"

"I never thought about it that way," Deon replied. As a matter of fact, while he attributed his success to positive role models and coaches who had helped him along the way, in reality it was his father who motivated his success. You see, sometimes people use bad experiences to make good things happen. This is one of the ways successes is able to live in the midst of the unforgiveness of a broken heart. This gentleman later stated it was this realization that was the turning point for him in therapy. Understanding that his anger towards his father was his inspiration and motivation opened his eyes to the secret motives hidden deep in his heart.

Everyone has a reason for doing the things they do. All of us are motivated by something. Christians normally like to believe that the biblical principles that underlie their moral belief system motivate them, but sometimes there are other things motivating good moral behavior. Motivators that hide themselves in 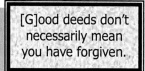 the deep dark chambers of unforgiveness sometimes mask themselves in good deeds. But good deeds don't necessarily mean you have forgiven. Here's how that played out for Deon:

After realizing the source of his motivation to succeed, this client was facing another dilemma. It dawned on him, as he continued to process these things, that there were serious issues of unforgiveness in his heart. He now faced one of the most critical crossroads of his life and enigmatic questions that left him cognitively paralyzed for some time, pondering how to go on.

With a disturbed look on his face as if to say he knew no other way to live, Deon said, "If I forgive my father, I won't have anything to motivate me, and I'll be left to being responsible for myself." He went on to say, "I've got something to prove and no matter what it takes for me to prove it, I'm willing to do that."

Can you imagine how many people are actually in Deon's situation? They have taken bad experiences and used those experiences to prove themselves to others, without ever addressing the underlying heart issue. Personal success does not necessarily mean you have overcome the pains of a broken heart, but forgiveness does. No level of success can heal the pains of a broken and unforgiving heart. And when you're motivated by anger or you are living to prove something to someone who hurt you, even if you reach a level that says, "I've made it," you really haven't, because your heart is still in so much pain. Material possessions and practical accomplishments only last for so long. Forgiveness lasts forever.

There are two ways to wage the resentment war. One is to outperform the person who hurt you; the other is to forgive that person. The first is rooted in pride, the latter in humility. Pride and humility serve as the interpretation filters of experience. Experiences interpreted with a prideful attitude will lean toward revenge and competition. You may hurt less on the outside, but your defense mechanisms leave you dying on the inside. Experiences interpreted by humility hurt more on the inside, but their authenticity sets you free to live on the outside. Many marriages end up with one partner desiring to show the other partner that they can make it without them. Business relationships sometimes end with partners in a competition to show who is superior. These are signs of unforgiveness and they can drive the works of good intentions to the depth of hurt and sorrow.

> There are two ways to wage ... war. One is to outperform the person who hurt you; the other is to forgive that person.

Let's go back to Deon, the young man who used his anger towards his father to accomplish good things. He was now in therapy and becoming more and more unhappy with how he had been manipulated by the schemes of his broken heart. Wonder why? He had been invited to go to therapy previously and had also had opportunities to mend his relationship with his father, but his subconscious mind knew that would kill his drive for success. What else would he use to drive himself if it wasn't anger towards his dad? In this very twisted and unhealthy way, he had unconsciously found justification for his feelings toward his father.

STAGE 5: Reconciliation

When asked why he was coming to therapy now, Deon broke down crying and said, "I want to love the man God chose to give me life through." Many years wasted, many days gone by, and now he realized that he had to do something he could have done a long time ago. It's never too late to choose forgiveness, and he was going to do just that. Deon elected to perform forgiveness surgery on himself!

In my work with Christian mentors and leaders throughout the nation, I have found that many of them train kids to be motivated by the things that have hurt them in life and to turn those negatives into positives. But I have rarely heard any talk about the damage it causes in the long run when forgiveness is not part of the equation. Children need to learn forgiveness and reconciliation. The way to success and maturity is not by the redirection of anger, but the resolution of it. Kids also need to learn to be motivated by the acts of biblical salvation and resolve the issues that may cause them to suffer forever on the inside.

> The way to success and maturity is not by the redirection of anger, but the resolution of it.

We all deserve the chance to be free from the motivation and worship of things that were intended to destroy us. Instead, we should be coached and mentored by the love that forgave us. Maybe it doesn't happen right away, but when it happens, it happens right. My mother used to say that anything good is worth working and waiting for. Be patient with yourself as you work through the anger you have towards others. Keep your hands to the plan as you get over the anger inside. Your freedom is drawing near.

There is no curing a sick man who believes himself to be in health. ~ Henri Amiel

CHAPTER 5

FORGIVENESS SURGERY

FROM DECISION TO DESTINY

Now that you've made the choice to forgive, you may begin the preoperative work needed to un-break the heart. This chapter will provide information on the rest of the process and prepare you for some of the challenges and joys that are ahead. Although it doesn't guarantee that you will feel better, it does come with the opportunity to process through your hurt and pain. It will also help you to begin to think seriously about getting on with your life. That's right: getting things done and embracing the hurts of the past by looking at them in a new way. You will begin to remember differently and learn how to develop new perspectives on past events.

Everyone deserves the opportunity to get on with their life without denying the events of the past. Through acceptance and being willing to go through the process, you will learn to genuinely reframe hopeless situations into hopeful situations and move on with your life – for real.

PRE-OP PROCEDURES

You may not feel like forgiving, or maybe you're willing to try doing it just to get through this book. Remember you don't have to feel it to do it. Forgiveness is one of those things where feelings and reality don't have to match. You can be in the process of forgiving someone and still feel angry. Here are a few things you should remember as you go through the phases of the forgiveness process:

1. You may vacillate between one phase and another. The most important thing is to know where you are. Self-awareness will help you understand and interpret how you may be feeling.

2. There is no time limit on this process. It can take days, months or even years. You don't have to rush it. Take your time. Forgiveness is a matter of the heart and no one can judge that but God *(But the LORD said to Samuel, "Do not look on his appearance or on the height of his stature, because I have rejected him. For the LORD sees not as man sees: man looks on the outward appearance, but the LORD looks on the heart." – 1 Samuel 16:7).* The only thing you can decide is how you respond and how you feel. The fruit of your social life is measured by who you have around you. So, share with your friends and your support system and be patient with yourself.

3. Be aware of defense mechanisms that may make it difficult for you to address issues related to forgiveness genuinely and honestly. A few defense mechanisms recognized in

psychoanalysis and psychodynamic theories are listed below to help you know what they are and how they affect you.

Displacement

Shifting your feelings from one person to another person, because the next person is more readily available and may be more accepting.

Denial

Acting like you don't feel what you feel, or that you are not in the situation you are in.

Distortion

Changing things around so they seem to mean something other than what they really mean; a misinterpretation of the facts.

Projection

Putting your feelings onto another person, telling them *they* feel or act a certain way because you don't accept those feelings and actions in yourself.

Passive Aggression

Using passive and subtle behavior to get back at someone who was offensive or aggressive towards you.

Repression

Not being able to remember certain things for the sake of alleviating or avoiding anxiety, impulses and ideals associated with the memory.

4. Seek professional help if you ever feel like ending your life or the life of another person for any reason. It is also suggested that you engage in a professional therapeutic relationship to help talk about some of these issues at a deeper and more personal level.

Patrick's Story

Patrick, a 25 year old male, came into my office because he was extremely angry with his father. His parents had divorced when he was about nine years old, his father moved to another part of the country and Patrick had limited contact with him while growing up. This did not seem to bother him during his early years, but as he entered his teens, he began to verbally express his anger towards his father and a desire to confront him. Patrick attributed his lack of contact with his dad to his father's being irresponsible and not caring to see him or be around him. He also blamed his father for abandoning him as a child.

When I asked Patrick if he loved his father, he immediately said no. I then asked him if he had *ever* loved his father, and he was surprisingly slower to say no. He actually said that he didn't know if he ever did. I explained to Patrick how unfortunate it was that he was never allowed to share a loving relationship with his dad. He grimaced at the words "unfortunate" and "loving relationship" as though they could never be used with the word "dad" in the same sentence. As we continued our discussion, Patrick began to discover that there were many people, including his mother, who actually had the opportunity to share a loving relationship with his father – an opportunity that was denied to Patrick.

I asked Patrick if he had ever asked his mother what it was like loving his father and again his answer was no. "Me and my mother don't talk like that," he said. I looked over at him and said, "How is it that others were allowed to love your father, but you were never given the chance?" As we continued to talk about his father, I realized that most of the people who knew his dad, according to Patrick, had pretty negative things to say about him. But even the people who talked bad about his father had spent time with him and the chance to love him. In the back of my mind I thought, "At least they had an opportunity to know him and to experience being with him in their life. Why wasn't Patrick given this chance?"

At that moment Patrick began to realize a deeper reality of his isolation and loneliness. It was becoming clear that he was missing something big. He never got time with his father that other people had. Patrick eventually said, "I never thought about it that way."

Honest and truthful beginnings can lead to hopeful endings. The Bible says that the truth will make you free. It also encourages us to tell the truth in love. Honesty promotes growth and insight in a person's life. The more honest you are, the more insight you will gain.

> Honest and truthful beginnings lead to hopeful endings.

To effectively forgive someone, you must acknowledge the truth about the situation. You have to be able to tell the story from a factual perspective. If you are a victim of abuse or betrayal, it may be difficult to acknowledge the truth without someone helping you through the process. It is sometimes hard to get to the truth on your own, because of the denial and repression defense mechanisms.

Once Patrick began looking for the truth from a different perspective, the emotions tied to his father began to unravel. He felt feelings of anger, not only towards his father, but also towards everyone else involved. He began to mentally balance his feelings, which gave way to a more productive and equal share of responsibility to all family members. Sometimes in these situations you have to realize that it's not only the absent father's fault; so many others can play a major role. Patrick soon learned that he was using anger to justify staying away from his father in an attempt to satisfy his broken heart. Once his attitude began to alter, this disparity also began to change into a possibility for hope and Patrick and his father began a long-delayed relationship.

Most of the shadows of life are caused by standing in our own sunshine. ~ Ralph Waldo Emerson

CHAPTER 6

PHASE I: REALIZATION

AWARENESS IS THE BEGINNING OF ALL THINGS

Many wonder if forgiveness is a principle or a process. There are strong arguments on both sides. If it is all principle, then why do some people say they forgive and then, years later, discover that just saying it didn't resolve the issues of their heart and now they find themselves in emotional pain? If it is all a process then it could take years to truly forgive someone and the common plea would be "give me time, I'm working on it."

I believe forgiveness is both a principle and a process. You have to be committed to do the difficult emotional work necessary to forgive and truly get over your broken heart.

In principle, forgiveness is required by God (*Bear with each other and forgive whatever grievances you may have against one another. Forgive as the Lord forgave you. – Colossians 3:13*). In process, it involves personal acknowledgements, resolution of anger and the restoration of hope. Remember, forgiveness has to do with helping love live.

The first phase of forgiveness is the **REALIZATION (Awareness) PHASE**. Awareness is recognizing when an injustice is done to you and realizing that you can't change what happened. It happened; it's over; and now it's time to go through the aftermath to get to the meaning. Realization is what takes place in the Confession Chamber of your heart.

> Awareness is recognizing when an injustice is done to you and realizing that you can't change what happened.

Regardless of what you have suffered in life, the simple fact that you are still breathing confirms that you made it through that very tough time. Still, when your body is out of a situation, sometimes your feelings can stay stuck there. I can't count the times I have had to remind clients in therapy that the event they found so painful had actually ended.

I have often used the analogy of a rainstorm. When you get caught in the rain unprepared, you are bound to get wet. And this time, it wasn't just a light shower; you were out in the kind of storm that knocks over buildings, flips cars and floods entire cities. I mean the kind of storm that leaves you treading water for days praying for God to rescue you because everyone else is gone. The kind of storm that leaves you drenched with water. The harder the rain, the wetter you get.

What most people don't consider is that, even when you manage to get out of the rain and reach a dry place, you're still soaking wet. You may not be caught in the storm any more, but you're still feeling the effects from it – the wetness – just as if you're still in the rain. But after a truly massive storm is over and the wind has settled; after the water has receded and flood water marks are left on the buildings; after the sun breaks through the clouds and the birds begin to fly again, the survivors appear. They may be wet and weary, but they are out of the storm and they know it is now time to do whatever needs to be done to recover from the catastrophe and get on with their lives.

Some of your family, friends and acquaintances may act like you should have it all together as soon as an incident is over. They forget that it often takes some time to dry off completely. But if you remember that just because you're still a little wet doesn't mean you're still in the storm, you'll be patient with yourself and not rush the healing process.

LEAVING "WELL ENOUGH" ALONE

Have you ever wished that something hadn't happened or that you had made different decisions that might have prevented things from happening the way they did? One high school student with low grades told me that he wished he could have started over and put more emphasis on making good marks. A woman married to a man with no prior history of child abuse, but who eventually abused her daughter, blamed herself for the incident, stating that, if she had not married him, the abuse would not have happened.

At some level, we all have experiences that leave us rethinking the decisions we made. But regardless of how we view things in retrospect, we can never change the reality that they happened.

To resolve the "could have... would have... should have" moments of life, you have to learn to deal with the realities. You have to face the things that happened with honesty. That's why when you go to a doctor, his or her first

> The closer you want to get to the truth, the deeper you have to go and the more honest you have to be.

question is, "What's going on?" The more accurate you are in telling the truth and giving specifics about what happened or what your symptoms are, the more the doctor will be able to help you. Think about that for a second. The more honest you are about your situation the better able your treatment provider is to help you. The power to survive is in your ability to give the most accurate information. It's the difference between the X-ray, and the CAT scan. The closer you want to get to the truth, the deeper you have to go and the more honest you have to be.

It is sometimes very hard to accept reality. Reality is like a mirror that stands in front of you showing you very clearly who you are. It reflects clearly what it sees and doesn't distort its image. It calls a spade a spade and doesn't apologize for it. In the movie, "A Few Good Men," Tom Cruise was cross-examining Jack Nicolson in court concerning the death of some soldiers. When Nicolson asked what he wanted from him, Cruise replied, "I want the truth!" Nicholson's response was, "You can't handle the truth!"

On the one hand, we want to get to the bottom of things, but on the other, we want to avoid what we might find. The truth is often very hard to accept and may also be very difficult to handle. We are prone to create stories and distort reality to make things seem better

> We are prone to create stories and distort reality to make things seem better than they really are.

than they really are. In doing so, the information needed for genuine forgiveness to take place is never gathered and the hope of getting better remains dormant in our heart for long periods of time.

One of the saddest sights in relationship counseling is when neither person in the relationship takes responsibility for their part in the struggle. This puts the relationship in quicksand where it is quickly pulled further and further down. As soon as a couple takes responsibility and begins dealing with the truth, they are rescued and pulled to safety. I think that all true healing of the heart must deal with the reality of the situation that caused it to hurt in the first place and that can be one of the greatest challenges of the whole process. Ask yourself, is your relationship important enough that you are willing to face the truth and accept it? Can *you* handle the truth?

Julia's Story:

Julia and her husband were always fighting. In counseling she mentioned that sometimes the fights got really bad, and she ended up with a black eye and missed days of work to allow time for her eye to heal. After hearing her story, I reflected by saying, "Julia, you've been abused for a long time." She was surprised that I had used the word "abused." She considered it just fighting and never saw it as abuse. In defending herself, she continued to try to convince me that the pair only fought; she justified it by the fact that her mother and father fought a lot, too. She said, "That's what we call it. That's what we've always called it."

Since Julia fought back when attacked by her husband, she considered it a fight, when in reality she was defending herself from abuse. As I continued to probe, she began to realize that the black eyes, missed days of work, sprained wrist and scars on her body were the results of abuse and not just fights the couple mutually engaged in. She began to realize that, even if they were fights, she lost most of them. She also hid this from close family members and friends. When asked why, she broke down in tears and said, "Because I didn't want Mom to know. I've always wanted to be different than her. I used to say that when I got married, I would never let a man do to me what she allowed Dad to do to her."

After a slight pause she admitted, "My situation is worse." Her tears and voice were like sighs of release from the denial that had held her captive for so long. To imagine that her personal life history had the power to keep her in such a dangerous situation was astounding.

After putting her head in her hands for a while in silence, Julia straightened up with confidence, wiped her tears, and made two statements that changed the course of her life forever. First, she acknowledged that her married life was just like her mother's, possibly worse. Secondly, she stated that she was being abused and not just fighting. She went on to declare that she didn't care who knew about it or what they thought about her, she would begin discussing her situation with other people, starting with her mother.

After a brief separation and treatment for her husband, the couple was able to get back together. They continue to be involved in both individual and family therapy.

In order to effectively deal with issues concerning forgiveness, you've got to start in the right place. You have to become aware of what happened and how you feel about it. Denial will only lead to more difficult emotional results. You've got to be honest and not be fearful of addressing the facts and telling the truth. And then you've got to learn to "let bygones be bygones." That means there are times in your life when you've got to tell what is gone, "Good-bye."

GATHERING INFORMATION

Awareness is all about information gathering – what happened, and how it is affecting you and your relationships. Remember, you're not committing to anything, you're just gathering the facts. Remember the old TV show, "Dragnet" and the line Sargent Joe Friday was supposed to have said? "Just the facts, ma'am."

You are doing a good self-study. You recognize that an injustice has been done to you and you make no excuses for it. Talking to people and asking questions helps you to get your facts straight. Rethinking through what happened from beginning to end helps you to put the story in order and in the right perspective. This could take some time, so be patient with yourself. How much time you need to spend gathering the facts will be determined by how long ago an event happened or how long it lasted. I often say that it is good to put the incident under a microscope to see the details of what happened. You don't have to draw any conclusions or make any assumptions at this stage, just simply journal the facts. Getting this information in order will help you identify where your heart was broken.

WHO'S RESPONSIBLE?

You are never responsible for someone abusing you or taking advantage of you. Even if you consider yourself weak, vulnerable or naïve, that still does not give people the right to abuse or take advantage of you. Your offender is fully answerable for what they did.

> You are never responsible for someone abusing you or taking advantage of you.

But often people who have been broken-hearted think that they are responsible for what happened to them. They blame themselves for the entire situation. Children who are victims of sexual and physical abuse are particularly prone to thinking they are the cause of it when, in reality, they are innocent victims. Children of divorced parents may often

61

feel that they caused their parents' separation. Many women in abusive relationships feel that if they would just do everything the way their abuser wants them to, they could keep the abuse from happening.

The truth of the matter is that you are not responsible for the physical and emotionally destructive behavior of others. The person who hurt you, left you, or cheated on you, did it because they chose to do so. They made an independent decision to break your heart, and they are wholly responsible for it.

As you begin to think about forgiving someone, allow yourself the freedom to blame them for the whole deal. At this stage that is very important, because it gives you the opportunity to identify the root causes in your heart. It may be hard initially, especially if you are in the habit of blaming yourself, but it will help you later as you get into the other phases of the forgiveness process.

NAMING WHO HURT YOU

Names give meaning to experience. They are like old songs that connect you to certain events in your life. That's why we stop using the names of people who hurt us. At one time you couldn't wait to hear it, and now you can't stand saying it.

Titles like "my baby momma" or "my baby daddy" are not just references to old relationships. They often reflect a deeper issue related to unforgiveness or unresolved issues in the relationship. When people are hurt in relationships they normally have a difficult time using the name of the person who hurt them. When a person's heart has been broken, they use any reference they can to avoid saying the name because names are intimate and personal. They refer to them as this guy, or that girl or use some other title to identify the person.

In a healthy relationship, a partner's name is often used to express intimate connection. It once felt good to say that person's name, but as the relationship went bad, it became harder to say the name affectionately the way you used to. How difficult it is to use a person's name often depends on the depth or level of the heartbreak.

Using vague titles allows you to mentally escape the hurtful elements of the relationship. Not using a name helps you to avoid the pain associated with the event.

Sometimes just hearing that person's name makes you cringe. But names help to build awareness in the forgiveness process. They help you establish connections between events and people. Remember, your hope for something different had to do with both the experience and the people involved.

Tim's Story:

Tim, for example, was a corporate executive who had been with his company for 25 years. An opportunity for promotion came up and a younger executive, Bailey, was given the position. Bailey only had 10 years of experience with the company and was at a lower position in the company than Tim. When the company promoted Bailey over Tim, Tim became furious. His resentment towards the people at the company began to overwhelm him and both his job and family began to be affected. He wanted revenge; and he also wanted find out how the company had made its decision, because he knew he was a man of good character, good leadership ability and very skilled in his trade.

I'll never forget Tim's first session. He came into the office and began to talk as though I was going to be his attorney. He was planning a legal pursuit against the company in his session with his therapist! After nearly 40 minutes, when he finally took a breath, I interrupted to said, "Tim, I'm your therapist, not your attorney." Even though legal counsel may have been appropriate, he had scheduled an appointment for therapy. When I said to him that he might have scheduled with the wrong office (a counselor rather than an attorney), he exclaimed, "I gave this company everything! All I had to offer went to this company!"

Tim went on to explain how much profit he brought into the company and how he was the creator and designer for many of the company's new initiatives. Then he used the words that told me he was a good candidate for emotional open-heart surgery – the surgery of forgiveness. He said, "My heart is so broken."

Tim was a Christian and he knew that what he was feeling and thinking was not what he *wanted* to be feeling and thinking. By our third session, we were moving away from vague explanations and towards specifics. Our conversation went something like this:

Tim: The company always treats people like they need them or something. They don't care about people. How long you've been there. How hard you work. It's just sad.

Me: Sad for you?

Tim: Well not only for me but also for a lot of other people. But they have really done me wrong now. Even other people in my department and throughout the company know that I should have been given that position.

Me: What other people?

Tim: Oh just people I work with.

Me: Like?

Tim: Everybody.

Me: You mean every single person in the company thinks you should have gotten that position?

Tim: Well, not everybody, but most of them.

Me: Who's saying you should have gotten it?

Tim: Well, Jack, he's been working with me for 15 years, as well as Tammy. Even the Vice President knows I'm more qualified for the position. They just did me so wrong.

Me: They?

Tim: Yeah, the company. God I hate that company!

Me: The whole company?

Tim: No, just the people who don't want me to advance. They have their people picked. Part of me feels like I just need to retire from it and do something different.

Me: Who doesn't want you to advance?

Tim: Do I need to say their names?

Me: For some reason, it seems hard to use their names. You've called them "the company," which makes it seem like more than 500 people hurt you.

Tim: No, it's not 500 people. It's Jack.

Me: Jack?

Tim: God, I really hate even saying his name.

Me: (smiling) His name is Jack.

Tim: Yep, Jack (laughing) Old Jack, Mr. Jack (shaking his head).

Me: What did Jack do?

Tim: Ja-a-ck... ... ...

As you can see, it took some time to get Tim to move from saying "the company" to stating exactly "who" in the company hurt him. That is exactly how we respond to situations when we are hurt. Sometimes my clients and I spend several sessions just getting to the identity of the person or people who broke their heart.

EXERCISES

Forgiveness Phase I – Awareness
Assignment 1:

Take time to go through this assignment by answering the questions. The exercises should be done in sections and over the course of a few days to give you some time to reflect on your questions and answers. Use the exercises in the order they are assigned.

1. State in simple clear words what happened.

2. How did it happen? Write the entire story.

3. When did it happen?

4. Where did it happen?

5. How did it make you feel?

6. Who was involved and what was their specific role in the event? Write their name(s).

7. Describe how it feels to write about the event and to name the person or persons who caused it.

8. What does it seem like the overall offense was?

9. How has it impacted your life?

10. What part of the event do you feel you could have controlled?

11. What do you feel you had no control over?

12. Whose fault do you feel it is? Why?

13. Who did it? Write their name(s) – again!

14. Who did it? Write their name(s) one more time.

15. If there was more than one event, or a range of events, repeat the exercise for each event.

Forgiveness Phase I – Awareness
Assignment 2:

Write your offender(s) a brief letter, naming them and blaming them for every detail of the hurtful event. Give them full responsibility for it and write it as though you were being given one last chance to tell them how you really felt.

1. Write the letter in as much detail as you can. Write it as though no one else will read it. Be honest and tell the truth about what happened.

2. After writing out the story, how do you feel about what happened?

3. How has this feeling been affecting you since the incident?

4. Read the following scriptures and spend some time praying about and absorbing their reality.

   Scripture 1: *I praise You because I am fearfully and wonderfully made; Your works are wonderful, I know that full well. (Psalm 139:14)*

Bad experiences can make you feel like you are not *fearfully and wonderfully made.* How has this happened in your life?

Scripture 2: *Before I formed you in the womb, I knew you, before you were born, I set you apart; I appointed you as a prophet to the nations. (Jeremiah 1:5)*

Sometimes you may have wondered if God was really aware of what you were going through. Or you may have wondered where He was. Explain your situation.

Scripture 3: *"For I know the plans I have for you," declares the LORD, "plans to prosper you and not to harm you, plans to give you hope and a future". – (Jeremiah 29:11)*

Hard times rarely feel like a blessing. How does this scripture assure you that God had your best interests in mind in your challenging situation? And, if He did, how do you feel you've "prospered" from that challenge?

Scripture 4: *A father to the fatherless, a defender of widows, is God in His holy dwelling. – (Psalm 68:5)*

Sometimes it's hard to perceive God (who you can't see) as a father, when you had a poor relationship with your biological father (who you could see). Explain your relationship with your father below and how that relationship impacted your life.

We cannot change the past, but we can change our attitude toward it. Uproot guilt and plant forgiveness. Tear out arrogance and seed humility. Exchange love for hate – thereby, making the present comfortable and the future promising. ~ Maya Angelou

CHAPTER 7

PHASE II: RECONCILING

THE MIRACLE OF MATCHING

The **RECONCILING (Matching) PHASE** is the second phase of forgiveness. While in the Awareness Phase you look for concrete clarity about the event or events that broke your heart, the Matching Phase takes the incident and matches it to the emotions it produced in you. For example, if someone has betrayed or hurt you and you felt and responded with anger, then we would discuss and match the event with anger. An angry response is a good example because it is the emotion most frequently associated with being broken-hearted. When you are successful at forgiveness, it helps to resolve anger and restore hope and purpose to your life.

Only when you understand the event and are able to clearly tell the story will you be ready to move to this phase. There may be times when parts of the story or incidents are completely blocked out. There may be segments of the event that you just can't remember. If remembering the details of events that have broken your heart seem overwhelmingly difficult, you may find that being in therapy helps.

Let's go back for a minute and talk about the big "E" – that's right, Emotions. Because in this phase you will have to know how your emotions work so that you can match them to the incident that broke your heart.

EMOTIONS

Most people just don't like to deal with emotions. They seem so complex and tricky. They interfere with every aspect of life and sometimes seem to get in the way of our good intentions. People wrestle with them, sometimes fighting to prevent them from showing their face inappropriately in situations. Emotions make us laugh, they make us cry and they give expression to life. Emotions are generated in the Reactive Chamber of your heart.

Losing your sensitivity to human emotions can be detrimental. Counselors have said that the lack of empathy can be a factor in motivating offenders to commit violent crimes. The less an individual is able to emotionally care about the well-being of others, the easier it is for them to harm them.

Emotions are important and feeling them is normal, even though we like to run and hide from the ones that make us feel uncomfortable. It is better to know what they are and what they feel like, than deny they exist and suppress them. The freedom of allowing yourself to feel your emotions helps you to better navigate through them.

Emotions do not think and make decisions; they only feel. I often jokingly say to clients who have had a hard time identifying with their emotions, "How are your feelers feeling today?" Ironically, that's a good example of how emotions work. They are just "feelers." Don't expect your emotions to do anything else.

These feelings let you know how things are going and help you navigate through life. An excessive amount of a particular emotion can lead to difficulty, such as high levels of anxiety or anger. Some people try to hide their emotions and resist the natural flow of feeling bad or at times even feeling good. I was counseling a couple once and the wife mentioned that her husband didn't show emotions. She assumed he had no emotions.

When he began to trust her with his feelings and vulnerability in therapy, she soon learned that he was full of emotions. He might have more emotions than she could even handle. Jokingly, she said, "Well, sometimes you have to be careful about what you ask for – you might just get it." And boy did she get an emotional load dumped on her as he began to vent the frustrations of his day and the other emotional struggles he was having. That's when you start thinking, "God, I wish he'd just sit with the remote and watch television."

Some people treat emotions like they are a big monster out to get them. Others think that the expression of them signifies a lack of control or weakness. Emotions are what they are and the way we use them in different situations makes all the difference. You have to have control over your emotions rather than letting them control you.

God gave emotions to you. He did not give you *to* emotions. They are a gift to you from God and he expects you to be a good steward of your emotions. I recall openly crying one day in a meeting with a group of preachers while discussing the difficulty I was experiencing in trying to start a Christian counseling center in a particular community. All the other preachers in the room discouraged me from crying and began to think that I had lost confidence in the whole project. But they had it wrong. What they did not know was that my genuine expression of hurt and discouragement was not a deterrent to reaching my objective, but rather made me stronger and more confident about completing the task.

Crying did not make me weak, but the strength gained in weakness made me cry. A genuine expression of vulnerability becomes the opportunity for you to really experience God's work

> Crying did not make me weak, but the strength gained in weakness made me cry.

through you. *(For in Him we live and move and have our being... – Acts 17:28)*

I also realize the tremendous pain that many men must be in because they are unable to genuinely express hurt or fear. They have learned to wrestle back the flooding tears which then press heavily against their heart. I realize how free many of them want to be, at least free to be emotional. The mystery is not that we all have emotions; it's that we have a need to express them. But it's the expression of their emotions that becomes the difficult part for so many people.

Emotions have got to be balanced and well navigated. Just like money, they have to be dispensed with wisdom and poise. In order for that to happen, you first have to *give yourself permission* to express your feelings in an appropriate way.

Martha's Story:

One of my clients was very angry with her husband. She stated, "I could just beat him up." Well, it would have been inappropriate for her to physically attack him, but her emotions would not resolve themselves until she had acted them out. I gave her permission to beat a pillow instead.

As Martha hit the pillow, she initially began to laugh because it seemed so awkward. Then in just a few seconds her laughter subsided, and she hit and talked – hit and talked – and eventually began to cry, screaming and shouting as if the pillow was really her husband. Finally, she threw the pillow across the room, saying, "You're not even worth it. I feel sorry for you."

Giving her permission to beat a pillow really helped Martha to get her emotions out. You would be surprised how such a simple act can help to relieve pain and anger. The point is that you have to get comfortable with feeling your emotions, because they are going to come out, one way or another. The longer you hold them in, the more intense they will be when they do come out.

THINKING & FEELING

It is good to think about how you feel. One of the hallmark statements of counselors after someone expresses what happened to him or her is, "Tell me how that makes you feel." It's that connection that helps a therapist identify where clients are in making the connection between an event on the outside and the feelings on the inside. What do you think about how a situation is making you feel? How well do the things on the outside match what you're feeling on the inside? The better you identify how it feels on the inside, the better you will be able to decide what to do with what's going on outside. That's how you keep from losing your cool. Know the inside (how you feel) as well as the outside (the event that happened) and check your thinking to see how you understand it all. The real question that needs to be answered is: "What is your brain thinking about how your body is feeling." The better you are at answering that question, the slower you'll be at reacting to painful situations.

Earl's Story:

When I ask clients how they feel, they often tell me what they think instead. That's because it's easier to think than it is to feel, especially when the feeling is unusual or painful. Thinking about a feeling gives rise to creating interpretations of the feeling, but not really getting in touch with the

> When I ask clients how they feel, they often tell me what they think. That's because it's easier to think than it is to feel ...

feeling in its purest form. For example, a client was confronted by his wife because he was painting the house at a time that was inconvenient for the whole family. I asked Earl how he felt about the confrontation and his response was that he felt like she was trying to say she didn't really care and that he was stupid.

Both "not caring" and "stupid" are mental interpretations and not feelings. After 30 minutes of helping him get through his thinking and focus on his feelings, Earl finally was able to state that he felt "hurt." He asserted that he was actually trying to do her a favor and impress her with his hard work and determination to paint the room they had talked about getting painted for months. To add to that, it was Valentine's Day and he wanted to get it done before the day ended and present it as a gift to his wife. She obviously did not have this inside information and was expecting something else to happen for Valentine's Day, which led to her frustration.

The couple's attempts to resolve the issue only turned into arguments until Earl was able to express his real emotion and not just his thoughts. This changed the entire course of the conversation and made it much more productive. When he mentioned he was hurting she began to listen attentively. She also began to understand that little things can hurt big men. It all happened because they were willing to go deeper and transition from what they thought to how they felt.

INCREASING YOUR RANGE OF EMOTIONS

On my son's 13th birthday, I brought him a small dirt bike. It was his first dirt bike and I, as his daring and good father, wanted to teach him how to ride and shift the gears. But, to be honest, it was Dad who learned two important lessons!

In hindsight, I have to admit that I was basically trying to show off to my boy so he could see how much of a superman his father was. Well, as I took off and began shifting gears, I fell off the dirt bike, injured my knee and wound up at the hospital. I now tell fathers, there comes a time in every man's life when he just has to retire from some things. I was apparently getting too old for showing off on a dirt bike.

The doctor examined my knee and explained that it was not broken. He gave me a brace to wear for six weeks and said that my knee would heal on its own. After wearing that brace for about five weeks, I noticed that I was unable to fully bend or extend my knee. My range of motion had decreased so much, I had to begin physical therapy to slowly increase it.

Whether I was walking, sleeping or simply sitting down, my knee would only slightly bend and slightly extend itself. I had to adjust the way I got in the car, got out the car, the way I climbed steps and the way I got dressed because my range of motion had been affected by this trauma.

Although physical therapy was painful, it sure served to get my knee back to where I could eventually fully flex it. During that period of recovery, I often thought to myself that you never really know how much something means to you until you actually lose it. I was extremely thankful when I had a full range of motion again.

Well, what happens when our *emotional* range of motion is limited? When we only know how to respond to situations with a limited catalog of feelings? It was once said that most people live their lives only able to express three to five emotions. In most cases these emotions are anger, sadness, fear, joy or sorrow. Can you imagine living your entire life and only having the opportunity to express three to five emotions? That's almost like not living at all. And what that means is that in all of your interactions with others, you only know how to feel three different ways. People only get a part of who you are when you are limited in your feelings.

During my work with inner city youth, I quickly realized that some of them had a very limited range of emotions. If you accidentally stepped on their shoe, they would get mad, and if you told them good morning, they would get mad. Even their brief moments of laughter would eventually turn to anger. Their range of emotion stretched from anger to anger with nothing in the middle. We spent time with these young people helping them to expand their range, so that they would have a larger pool of emotions to draw from. And we were relentless, because we knew what a huge difference it could make in their lives.

When things happen to people, they have choices to make about how they feel as a result. These choices are conscious decisions that the brain makes based upon its familiarity with the range of their emotional categories. There are obviously very basic feelings that everyone at some level experiences, but the ability to express a wide variety of emotions most often needs to be learned. Yes, that's right – we have to teach ourselves how to feel different feelings so that when we run across situations in our daily lives, we have a broader selection to choose from.

Jimmy's Story:

Jimmy was a high school student who came to see me because his grades began to drop in school and his parents were concerned that he was becoming more and more depressed. During the six months that we worked together, Jimmy voiced how he felt life wasn't fair for him. His father left home when he was very young, and was now married to another woman raising their kids together. Jimmy had a 14-year-old stepbrother, Carl. Jimmy felt his father loved Carl more than he loved him because his father was with that family.

Jimmy had also lost a close friend in an accident and had no positive role models. He felt all alone. He was confused about so much. He would often come to the office and just sit in the chair for long minutes before even speaking a word. Or he would come in and just throw himself on the couch as though his days were long and hard. I would sometimes think to myself that he was a young man just doing what young men do. But the problem was that, internally, he was always trying to deal with a grown man's emotions and it was slowly becoming too much for him. It's hard for young people to deal with grown-up situations. Jimmy seemed tired and drained, but at the same time happy to be in counseling – a place he never thought he would be.

One day Jimmy became very angry with me in therapy. I had never seen him so angry and defiant. When I asked him why he was upset, he said it was because his father had the nerve to tell him *that he loved him*. I was astonished. In my mind that was something to be glad about, but I understood that anger was a powerful emotional category for Jimmy. It was an emotion he was familiar with; he knew it and it knew him. He could feel anger very easily without even thinking, but remorse, love and empathy were more difficult for him. These were unfamiliar emotions and were seldom expressed in any context. They were categories that needed to be built up and strengthened in his life.

It's one thing to love a hurting child, but it's another thing to teach that child to love others. The first is often the easier task. In order for people to reciprocate something, they must first own it for themselves. In Jimmy's case, he had to own the fact that he loved the thought of his father loving him. He had to own that the idea felt good. It was both secure and comforting

> It's one thing to love a hurting child, and it's another thing to teach them to love others.

and beyond everything else; it was real. Then he had to realize that he could feel his father's love as often as he allowed himself to do so. Together we worked on learning how he could give himself permission to expand and grow his emotional categories. I was delighted when he started calling this process, "The Lord, expanding His territory."

The more possibilities we have in the way we choose to feel, the better we will be able to get through situations and identify how they are emotionally affecting us. In other words, the better you are able to identify with how you feel, the more effective you will be in making healthy choices.

EXERCISES

Forgiveness Phase II – Matching
Assignment 1:

List below your three main feelings. These are the feelings you are most familiar and comfortable with. These are the feelings you know how to feel. These three emotions – whether we label them positive emotions or negative emotions – are your friends. In most situations, you choose one of these three to express yourself. Rank these feelings 1-3 on the lines to the right (1 = You choose this feeling most times / 3 = You choose this feeling least often).

FEELING   **RANK**

1. _____   _____

2. _____   _____

3. _____   _____

Now answer the following questions:

1. Which one of these three emotions did you feel the most when your heart was broken?

2. What happened that made you feel that way?

Forgiveness Phase II – Matching Assignment 2:

Let's look at other feeling possibilities. In doing so, we will try to increase your range of emotions. Below is a list of 114 different feelings. Take time and read through the list. After you have finished, go back through and circle your "Oh, yeah!" emotions (the ones you are *very* familiar with).

114 Emotions

"I feel ..."

Accepted	feeling of being regarded favorably
Accepting	open or welcoming
Agitated	troubled or nervous
Alarmed	anxious; frightened; aware of danger
Amused	entertained or laughing
Angry	feeling or showing anger
Angst	profound feeling of generalized anxiety or dread
Annoyed	pestered; harassed; attacked repeatedly
Anticipation	looking forward to or expecting
Anxiety	feeling of worry or unease; eagerness to do something
Apprehension	anticipation coupled with anxiety or fear

Apathetic	not interested, unenthusiastic
Aversion	strong dislike or disinclination
Awe	great respect, usually mixed with fear
Bitterness	feelings of anger, hurt and resentment
Boredom	weariness and disinterest in something considered as dull and tedious
Bewilderment	feeling of being perplexed or confused
Betrayal	feeling resulting from another's disloyalty or break of trust; often involving treachery
Calm	peaceful and not showing nervousness, anger or other emotions
Cautious	careful to avoid potential problem or danger
Closeness	feeling of being connected; united; bound together by strong relationship and common interest
Comfortable	enjoying physical comfort; at ease
Compassion	concern for the sufferings or misfortunes of others
Completeness	feeling of being whole; nothing more is needed
Contentment	a state of peaceful happiness or satisfaction
Confident	certain in oneself or about something
Confusion	bewilderment; lack of understanding
Constrained	held within bounds or compelled or forced towards a specific course of action

Courageous	brave; feeling able to handle danger or pain without appearing frightened
Depressed	feeling utterly dispirited or dejected
Disappointed	feeling sad or displeased because one's hopes or expectations were not fulfilled
Discontented	feeling a lack of satisfaction
Disgusted	strong revulsion or indignation
Desire	strong feeling of wanting to have something or wishing for something to happen
Delighted	very pleased
Determined	resolute; having firmness of purpose
Distressed	feeling extreme anxiety or suffering
Doubtful	uncertain
Drained	tired or used up completely
Embarrassed	feeling awkward, self-conscious or ashamed
Enjoyment	delight, taking pleasure in
Ennui	listlessness and dissatisfaction arising from boredom
Enthusiastic	feeling passionate enjoyment, interest or approval
Envious	resentful of another's qualities, possessions or luck and longing for the same
Euphoric	intensely happy; having an exaggerated feeling of well-being or elation
Fearful	afraid

Friendliness	bond of mutual, but not sexual, affection
Frustrated	feeling of being thwarted in attaining goals
Gleeful	feeling great delight
Glad	pleased; grateful
Grateful	thankful
Greedy	feeling intense and selfish desire for food, wealth or power
Grief	intense sorrow, especially that caused by someone's death
Guilt	feeling responsibility for a wrongdoing, fault or error
Hatred	feeling of intense dislike towards someone or something
Happy	feeling pleasure or contentment
Homesick	feeling upset because one is missing one's home
Honored	feeling of pride and pleasure from being shown respect
Hope	feeling of expectation and desire that something will happen
Horror	intense feeling of fear, shock or disgust
Humble	modesty or low estimation of one's own importance
Hurt	mental pain or distress caused by actions of another
Impatient	lacking patience or tolerance

Inadequate	unable to deal with a situation or life in general
Indignation	annoyance provoked by what is perceived as unfair treatment
Interested	wanting to know about something or someone
Irritated	annoyed
Isolated	feeling lonely and cut off from others
Joyful	feeling of great pleasure and happiness
Jealous	resentful of someone regarded as a rival (often sexual); fiercely fighting for attention
Lonely	sad because one has no friends or company
Love	feeling of deep affection; deep romantic or sexual attachment to someone
Lust	strong sexual desire, usually unaccompanied by love or compassion
Mad	angry; *or* (slang) extremely foolish or ill-advised or very enthusiastic about something
Melancholy	deep and long-lasting sadness
Modest	unassuming in the estimation of one's abilities or attributes; not prone to showing off
Naive	lacking experience, wisdom and judgment
Nervous	apprehensive; easily agitated or alarmed

Negative	undesirable; pessimistic; denial; expressing disagreement
Nostalgic	feeling a sentimental longing or wishful affection for the past
Pain	physical or mental suffering or distress
Panic	sudden uncontrollable fear or anxiety; informal frenzied hurry
Patient	having or showing patience; uncomplaining
Peaceful	free from disturbance; calm; inclined to avoid conflict
Phobic	feeling of irrational fear of something
Pity	feeling of sorrow and compassion caused by sufferings of others
Pleasure	feeling of happy satisfaction and enjoyment
Proud	feeling deep pleasure or satisfaction derived from one's achievements
Rage	violent uncontrollable anger
Regret	feeling of sorrow, repentance or disappointment regarding an event
Remorseful	feeling deep regret or guilt for a wrong committed
Resentful	feeling bitter or indignant about something someone else did or didn't do
Sad	unhappy; feeling sorrow
Satisfied	feeling pleasure at having met expectations, needs or desires

Self-pity	excessive concern with and unhappiness over one's own troubles
Shame	feeling of humiliation caused by awareness of wrong or foolish behavior
Shy	timid in the company of others; slow or reluctant to do something unfamiliar
Shock	feeling caused by sudden upsetting or surprising event or experience
Suffering	experiencing something bad, painful or unpleasant
Sorrow	sadness
Surprise	mild astonishment caused by something unexpected
Suspense	feeling of excited or anxious uncertainty about what may happen
Sympathetic	feeling empathy with or approval of an idea, action, sentiment or opinion
Terrified	feeling terror or extreme fear
Tired/tired of	feeling exhausted mentally or physically; drained; bored by or loss of interest in something;
Timid	shy and fearful, easily intimidated, unwilling to take risks
Troubled	worried; problematic
Trustful	having a firm belief in the reliability, truth, ability or strength of someone or something
Vulnerable	exposed to being attacked or harmed

Wonder	feeling of surprise or admiration caused by something beautiful or awe-inspiring
Worried	anxious or troubled over actual or potential difficulties
Wrathful	full of intense anger
Yearning	intense feeling of loss and longing for something
Zestful	filled with great enthusiasm and energy

This is obviously a long list, yet it does not reflect all the feelings a person can have.

How do you learn to expand your range of feeling possibilities? I would first say that it takes time. You have to be willing to commit to trying to feel differently and you have got to be patient. I have found that a cognitive approach to increasing your range of emotions works well for most people. My recommendation for learning a new feeling is to, first, think about the feeling and when and how it might show itself.

Then, as you identify with new emotions, try using new combinations of words to describe your feelings. Instead of saying things like, "I hate myself when I mess up," try saying, "I often feel impatient with myself." This will help nurture your personal convictions without condemning yourself.

Finally, choose at least one emotion that you are not familiar with and identify times when it would be appropriate to feel that emotion (assuming that it is not being expressed in a way that is injurious to you or other people). My suggestion is that you take one new emotion per week, get familiar with its meaning and identify the times you actually feel it. Over time you will develop a broader range of feelings that will help you deal with issues more effectively.

Forgiveness Phase II – Matching
Assignment 3:

The Matching Map

1. List below the **event** that happened, how it made you
    feel; how it made you **think** about yourself, and what it
    made you **do**.

EVENT (The Outside/Beginning)

_____

FEELING (The Inside)

_____

THOUGHT (The Middle)

_____

ACTION (The Outside/End)

_____

2. What are you beginning to notice about the relationship between the event, your feelings about the event and the way it impacted your thinking?

3. Certain defense mechanisms are used as blockers. They can be placed anywhere in the Matching Map. Make a list of the defense mechanisms you have used to block certain thoughts and feelings.

My Defense Mechanisms

1. _____

2. _____

3. _____

4. _____

5. _____

4. Now place your defense mechanisms on your Matching Map in the areas where they operate the most and describe how they try to protect you.

EVENT (The Outside/Beginning)

FEELING (The Inside)

THOUGHT (The Middle)

ACTION (The Outside/End)

Get mad, then get over it. ~ Colin Powell

CHAPTER 8

PHASE III: REDEMPTION

OPEN HEART SURGERY – CUTTING AWAY ANGER TO RESTORE HOPE

The **REDEMPTION PHASE is the third phase of forgiveness.** In Phase I, you accepted the trauma that happened to you; then you matched your emotions to that event and the person who broke your heart in Phase II. In this phase, you've going to put your anger under the knife. We will put anger on the examination table and take a long, hard look at all the ways it presents itself, from mild annoyance to uncontrolled rage and longing for revenge. It is in Phase III that most of the therapeutic work related to resolving anger takes place.

"Redemption" is from the Latin meaning to redeem, buy back, exchange or reclaim. This phase has to do with regaining emotional strength, resolving issues related to anger, reframing hurtful experiences, and restoring self-confidence, which is often diminished when the heart is broken.

REGAINING EMOTIONAL STRENGTH

Let's begin with regaining insight and emotional strength. The need for emotional strength presupposes emotional weakness, meaning that at some point you allowed an emotion to take control of your heart and impact the way you acted. This happens when a person allows their feelings to control their behavior over a long period of time. Sometimes it is done consciously and at other times it happens without your even being aware of it. When emotions have control over you, you have to work on rebuilding your emotional strength (ability to control emotions).

Another way to look at uncontrollable emotions is to consider them untamed. It's like taking an animal from the wild and raising it in your home. It has to learn the rules of living in its new home with its new family. Untamed emotions bleed from the wound of a broken heart and the more you try to prevent them from showing, the stronger they get. You have to strategically begin to work on developing the emotional muscle necessary to regain control over untamed emotions, so that they are not controlling you, but you are controlling them.

> You have to [develop] the emotional muscle necessary to regain control over untamed emotions...

Emotions need muscle (strength) to be tamed. Without strength, they just bounce around doing whatever they want to do. It's like the relationship between the waters of the river and the banks that bend it towards the ocean. The banks of the river hold it in check and direct its flow. But when the river floods, like untamed emotions, they overflow the banks and go where they will. We need to help you shore up the banks and make them strong, so they can hold in the river of your feelings to go where *you* want them to go.

During the trauma you experienced, you may not have had the emotional muscle needed for your anger to be tamed by your brain. It does what it wants, when it wants, and you suffer the consequences for its actions. So let's take anger to the emotional gym and work it out, focusing on building muscle so that you can contain it, instead of allowing it to hurt you and others. You want to give your anger a special diet so that it feeds on the things that help it grow healthy, rather than make it more uncontrollable.

I must reiterate that the emotion most associated with a broken heart is anger, so that is the one we will concentrate on during your open-heart surgery. You may say that you have been feeling more anxiety and depression than anger, but the root of those emotions are probably still anger that hides itself behind depression or anxiety. If you deal with the anger, you resolve the depression and anxiety.

Depression is often defined as anger turned inward. When you think about it logically, you see that anger is the most logical emotional response to a broken heart. You were hurt or violated, giving you a legitimate right to be angry. If you don't take charge and manage your anger, it will lead to damaged health, relationships, job and many other areas of your life.

The thing is, anger is not meant to control you; it is an emotion that can actually give you an opportunity to effectively navigate through life.

THE FACES OF ANGER

Anger is caused by physical or emotional pain. It is an automatic response to pain. It is usually triggered by thoughts that someone is trying to hurt you. When your heart breaks, anger wakes up and goes to work – often behind the scenes, hiding its face in other emotions and beginning to take the remaining life out of your broken heart.

Anger is a normal emotion, not necessarily a bad emotion. *(In your anger do not sin... – Ephesians 4:26).* A lot of people are uncomfortable with anger. They feel that any display of the slightest anger means that they are weak or out of control, cruel or heartless, so they suppress their anger, which actually makes things worse for them. In Tyler Perry's "Diary of a Mad Black Woman," Helen carried some of the problems associated with her anger into a new relationship with Orlando. Leaving her former relationship wasn't enough. She had to relearn love in a new way. Her anger and her fears kept getting in the way of her future. Sometimes the past can be so bad that it prevents you from seeing the possibilities of your future. Accepting her anger and working through it cleared the way for a brighter future for Helen, and a better and safer relationship. Had she not accepted her condition, she couldn't have corrected it. That's why you have to give yourself permission to be angry first if you want to move on to resolving your anger. You can't resolve something you don't admit to having.

Anger can be used constructively or destructively. You can use your anger to accomplish positive things, rather than suffer the negative consequences of destructive and aggressive acts towards others. Regardless of how it is used, anger still has to be resolved or you will continue to have problems. Like Deon in Chapter 4, the person who has learned to use their anger constructively will still one day have to face the music and deal with the source of that anger. It is better to do it earlier in life than later. And because anger is so tricky, its signs are not always explosive events acted out with violence. It expresses itself in other ways as well, such as silence, withdrawing, being late, overly dramatized (but insincere) friendliness and similar forms of covert manipulation.

Even though you don't see the signs of your anger, that doesn't mean you are not angry.

The expression of anger is a choice. Yep, for all of you who would like to blame anger as justification for your actions – sorry. The *feeling* of anger may be involuntary, but the *expression* of anger is a choice. You have to decide how you are going to express the feeling, or whether you are going to outwardly express it at all. A client once tried to convince me that he was not angry about a situation in his life. He told me that he had gotten over the situation, but all the while he was scratching his head, moving around in his chair and flapping his feet as he told the story. He was like a time bomb getting ready to explode any minute. He had not developed the skills necessary to express his anger effectively. When you don't develop a constructive pattern of expressing anger, you are left with the destructive alternative that anger creates on its own.

Anger can be lonely. An angry person is a lonely person. Regardless of how many friends they may have or how many events they attend, deep down inside they feel empty and lonely. Anger doesn't create socialization and life. It creates separation and death. It doesn't 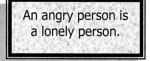 promote healthy relationships, but tears them down. It doesn't help build your self-esteem, but tears away at your confidence, eventually pulling you into an emotional hole too deep to jump out of by yourself. Accepting this loneliness as inevitable as you work through your anger is actually a positive step. Give yourself time as you work through the loneliness of anger. It's hard for people to empathize with situations they haven't been in themselves, so don't expect them to understand you right away.

Anger wants you to make excuses for it. It dreads taking responsibility for itself. It wants to act out and then blame other people for the results.

Tony's Story:

Tony got mad at her boyfriend because he cheated on her. She then came up with the brilliant idea to retaliate by cheating on him. Of course, her cheating didn't resolve anything for her; it only made her life worse. When I asked why she cheated, she said she wanted to get back at him and let him feel what she felt. The problem was that she wasn't feeling any better being with someone else, knowing she was doing it only to get back at her boyfriend. In the end, she blamed the boyfriend for her cheating and for her new relationship going bad. Everything that went wrong in her life was him, him, *him*. Tony later understood that she had "stooped" to his level and had accomplished nothing in doing so. All she gained was another very confusing relationship.

But that was a choice she made, not just a mistake she stumbled into. That's why, when you find yourself feeling anger at another person, you have to take your time and be patient with yourself. People may have rushed you into things all your life and now your emotions are trying to rush you into feeling a certain way and wanting to blame others for it. Take control of yourself – and let both people and your emotions know that you, not they, will be in charge from here on out.

Anytime a person feels controlled by their anger it makes them powerless to change it and this just makes them angrier. Being controlled and feeling controlled causes anger that you may or may not be able to be express. And since anger can last for such a long time, it is important to get things straight in your thinking and feelings as soon as you can.

Anger likes it when you are mad. It will try to do everything it can to keep you mad. One of its greatest strategies is having you blame others for your problems. In fact, the only way to stay mad is to blame others. When you actually start looking at situations to see where you fit in or determine what role you played, that's a good sign that you are beginning to heal from your anger. You no longer blame others, but start taking responsibility for your own actions.

Anger can look like depression. Anytime you exhaust your emotional energy by expressing your anger towards another who hurt you, it makes you tired. It literally drains you. The energy that could be used to help you get through the hurt is all being used to be angry with the person instead. I mean you wake up mad, you work mad, you think mad, you eat mad, you sleep mad and then you wake up again – *mad.*

But when you've finally exhausted yourself sending anger towards another person, it just turns inward in the form of sadness and depression. You begin taking the feelings out on yourself, wasting time and losing sleep over it. The more this anger is turned inward, the more depressed you become.

Anger wants to change the situation quickly. Anger wants to turn the tables around to make the perpetrator the victim and make the victim the victor. It wants to do this by all means possible. So you make that other person a little god in your life without even realizing it and do everything you can to show them that they didn't get the best of you. Anger doesn't want to negotiate who's right and wrong, it just wants to win. Its objective is to get out of pain and get rid of it fast.

Anger is a weapon that works against forgiveness, yet it is because of anger that you need to forgive. When you decide to forgive, you basically arrest anger and slow it down. You put it in a state of shock and you take control of your life. Anger knows forgiveness puts the breaks on its energy, but it wants revenge by any means necessary and it will

> Anger ... wants revenge by any means necessary.

fight to keep moving forward. It's like holding the accelerator and the breaks down on a car at the same time. It creates a lot of noise, a lot of jerks and bumps, but the car doesn't go anywhere. It's just burnt-up energy, burnt rubber and smoke, creating a cloud that it simply loses itself in.

THREE TYPES OF ANGER

SUPPRESSED ANGER – Have you ever met someone who holds his or her anger in all the time? You have probably seen them in situations where you knew they were angry, but they denied it. Suppressed anger is like taking your feelings and hiding them from your own self. People who suppress their anger sometimes don't even know they're angry until they are put in a situation that forces them to acknowledge it. I once used an empty chair in a therapeutic session to help a client express suppressed anger. By having the empty chair next to her representing the person she had identified as the one who broke her heart, I was able to help her do two things. The first was to realize that she still had a lot of anger inside of her concerning that person. Suppressed anger will eventually come out; it's just a matter of time. The second thing this allowed her was the opportunity to get her anger out in an appropriate way. When suppressed anger begins to surface, a person may not even know what they are mad about and just seem to have an angry attitude towards the world in general.

PROJECTED ANGER – I'm sure you heard the story of the man who was mad at his wife and kicked the cat. Projected anger is when you are mad at one person, but you take it out on another. People project their anger on others for several different reasons. Sometimes it's easier to express anger at one person than the other. Sometimes one person is closer to them emotionally. A husband who gets mad at his boss may come home and project that anger onto his wife and children. A woman abused by her former husband may project her anger towards her current husband. People who project their anger onto others normally have a difficult time resolving conflict and effectively communicating.

TWISTED ANGER – Twisted anger is anger that is sometimes upside down. It has learned to present with positive behaviors, but behind those behaviors there is violence and rage. Earlier you read about Deon, the young man who went to college and accomplished a lot in life because he was angry with his father. Because of their success and accomplishments, people with twisted anger are some of the most difficult to convince that they are still angry. I've heard coaches say that they wanted to channel a youngster's anger into athletics. That's an example of how anger can get twisted. Channeling anger from one object to another doesn't resolve it. Working through anger resolves it.

RESOLVING YOUR ANGER

1. Own your anger

My grandmother always said that, if it walks like a duck and quacks like a duck, it's probably a duck. What she meant by that was that you have to be honest with yourself and recognize the truth in a situation. You have to tell yourself the truth and accept responsibility for your actions and your feelings.

<u>Justin's Story:</u>

A friend of mine is a teacher for a private Christian school. He had worked very hard during the course of his teaching career and had been able to effectively assimilate into mainstream teaching circles of some of the most distinctive educators and administrators. However, there was one incident that was very hurtful for him. When Justin, who is black, taught at a school staffed with predominately white administrators, he experienced racism and discrimination, which lead to him to leave the school. When I asked him about the situation, he very persuasively said, "Oh that was no big deal. That was not bad at all." But our further discussion revealed the discouragement and pain that incident had caused him.

In order to genuinely forgive someone, you can't make excuses for them. You have to be honest about what they did and let them have full ownership for it. During a conversation with Justin, I told him how sorry I was that he had that experience. He began to cry; but he also began to express a new feeling – a feeling of freedom that eventually gave him permission to deal effectively with the anger that he held in for so long.

Give yourself permission to be angry. Suppressing anger only leads to depression and other problems.

2. Learn to relax

Stop being so dependent on others accepting and loving you and going by your rules. Just because you feel like you lost something in a past you couldn't control, doesn't mean you have to control everything now. Ask yourself, "Why must I control the details, when, in reality, I ultimately control nothing?" And by the way, no one really cares that you are mad. Have you ever noticed that, while you're mad and disgruntled about things, other people are going about their normal routine? Your anger doesn't scare anyone and doesn't intimidate anyone. If anything, it just makes people not want to be around you. You are just wearing yourself out – always tense, tight and pressured. Relax, things will get done. Often we find that the more tensed and pressured we are, the harder it is to truly depend on God.

Relaxation Bible Scriptures

Proverbs 15:1

Matthew 5:21-24

Romans 12:17-21

Ephesians 4:26-32

James 1:19-21

Anne's Story:

Anne and her teenage son came to counseling because the boy was not taking care of his responsibilities and she could not get him to do anything in a timely manner. Anne was concerned because Smitty, her son, was getting ready to go to college soon and she wanted to make sure he could handle independence. Initially, she complained that he didn't clean his room, throw out the trash, get his clothes

---

Seven Ways to Relax

1. Practice relaxation techniques

2. Slow down and get your facts straight

3. Put yourself in timeout

4. Count to 10 – calm down, then act

5. Talk to yourself

6. Try imagery therapy in counseling

7. Exercise healthy breathing practices

---

ready, etc. I sat there wondering out loud who was doing all this stuff if he wasn't. Anne admitted that she was and that if she didn't do it, it would not get done because Smitty simply didn't care.

Although she was astonished when I said to her, "Stop doing it," Anne gave it a shot and miraculously her son began to do his chores without prompting. What lesson had she learned? First, sometimes when you want people to do something for themselves, you have to stop doing it for them. And secondly, she realized that life would go on and things would get done, even if she didn't do it. The sun didn't rise and set on whether she was able to make things happen or not. So she learned to relax.

Listen, calm down for God's sake. Relaxing and practicing relaxation can help you discover new ways of handling situations that now cause you to become angry.

3. Watch your thinking

Monitor the movement of your thoughts as they influence how you feel and eventually how you act. Remember, the cycle is interactive: Feelings → Thoughts →Action → Thoughts → Feelings → Action. Thoughts will become feelings; feelings evolve into passionate urges and those passionate urges have two possibilities: they can either be withheld or they can be released to action. Eventually feelings become the fuel that prompts your thoughts and thoughts become the fuel that prompts your feelings. They learn to engage with each other to justify and validate the actions produced.

Ask yourself, "Where is my thinking leading me?" You have to get ahead of your thinking and see where it's going to take you. That way you can run back and divert it in another direction. One thought leads to one feeling and that feeling leads to an action; the action leads to another thought, which leads to a new feeling and so on and so on. Your eventual actions are based on your feelings which are based on your thoughts. But we never know exactly when that action will occur.

Monica's Story:

For example, Monica, a client who was starting to pay more attention to her thinking, made this statement in one of her therapeutic exercises: "When I get frustrated, I feel unwanted and when I feel unwanted I get angry; when I get angry I lose it, when I lose it someone gets hurt; when someone gets hurt, I feel sorry and when I start feeling sorry, I begin to blame myself for everything and begin to feel hopeless; and when I start feeling hopeless, I get mad at myself and when I get mad at myself, I…"

You can see how her thinking and feeling cycle unfolded because she was able to follow how thinking and feeling worked together to lead to actions. The good thing was that Monica was so in touch with her feelings and her thinking, that it was easy to help her get ahead of herself to block those thoughts, feelings and actions that could be self-destructive and possibly harmful to others.

Let me repeat: although the feeling of anger is automatic, the expression of anger is a choice. It is a cognitive choice that happens in the brain. Regardless of what anger feels like, choosing the right action can control the expression of it. That's why you are always responsible for the way you express your anger. You can never blame others for what you do or say in anger. That's your choice and you control it. The bottom line in learning to resolve and manage your anger is to know that you have to match your feeling with your thinking. And because anger and depression can be expressed in the same way at times, you have to be able to know which one you're really dealing with.

> Although the feeling of anger is automatic, the expression of anger is a choice.

I was always reminding my oldest son to think before he acts. In essence, there is a space between feeling and acting where thinking has the ability to fully influence action. Boy, does that put you in total control! No more "knee-jerk" reactions. As much as anger would like to control you, it really can't because in the middle of it all, you and your brain have the final say. Isn't that good news?

Because anger is fueled by your thoughts, it can be resolved through restructuring the way you think about a situation. In the space between the actions that hurt you and the way you respond is the very delicate opportunity for thinking. That's right, thinking happens in that tiny gap.

We will use the acronym **S.T.O.P.** to help us respond to situations that make us angry. Remember to **S.T.O.P.** when things make you angry so that you can respond appropriately and not just react to your feelings. The **S.T.O.P.** acronym will help you fill in the details in that thinking-feeling space between what happened and how you react to it.

1st: **S**   Situation assessment – "What just happened?"

2nd: **T**   Thoughts about a situation – "What am I thinking and how am I feeling about this?"

3rd: **O**   Order of a situation – "What are the detailed events of the situation?"

4th: **P**   Plan – "How should I interpret the situation based on the information I've gathered?"

Here's one way you can change your thinking: earlier we talked about naming the person who hurt you and focusing on how the person treated you. Now we want to move away from the person and towards the event. This transition helps you to think of the *act* as being the violator rather than the person performing the act. Anger should be directed at the event and not the person. This helps to put things into the proper perspective.

If they try to control their reaction at all, most people make the mistake of attempting to stop the process at the feelings stage. They suppress their feelings or begin acting like they don't feel a certain way. But, because feelings can only be stuffed for a limited time, this only causes the emotions to pile

> Thoughts trapped
> in your brain
> struggle ... to find
> freedom in action.

up until one day that person explodes in emotionally charged and usually inappropriate action. Thoughts trapped in your brain struggle (through feelings) to find freedom in action. When you try to block feelings, you do yourself an injustice. But by pausing in the process at the *thinking* level, you can change your feelings which then can lead to appropriate, healthy actions.

So remember to **S.T.O.P.** before you react to a situation that has caused you to be angry. Anger does not control you, but you control it. The objective is to alleviate anger and have better control over your emotions.

4. Watch your life

Live within your emotional means. Stop setting yourself up for emotional distress or you will find yourself in the negative column in your feelings account. Being emotion-

> Live within your emotional means. ... Being emotionally withdrawn in your feelings account is like being in the negative in your checking account

ally overdrawn on your feelings account is like being in the negative in your checking account with pending checks still due to clear. It only causes more worry, more anxiety and more stress.

Paying more attention to the way you live will help you prevent overextending yourself in your emotional account. Sometimes people are so accustomed to living in an atmosphere of negativity that they don't even realize they are doing negative things, thinking negative thoughts, feeling negative feelings and being overwhelmed with negative surroundings and negative energy. Think about it this way: the relationships we normally engage in reflect the way we feel about ourselves. If the environment you are in is not the environment you desire, it's up to you to change it.

Maria's Story

There are several ways to ensure that you don't over extend yourself in your emotional life. I remember working with a single mother who had two sons. Maria loved both of her boys equally, but it seemed as though most of her attention was given to Tommy, who was always getting in trouble. Maria was always stressed out and complaining about the problems this son gave her, but she was always attentive to him. Eventually, the other son, Darrell, learned that being good didn't get him much attention, so he started misbehaving as well. Maria now had *two* recalcitrant sons to deal with.

After a few sessions, Maria realized that in some weird way she had been programmed to reward negative behavior by paying more attention to negative things than positive things. As a result, she now had another misbehaving child because the children learned that bad behavior got Mom's attention. Paying attention to where you put your energy will help you learn how not to waste it on negative things.

5. Serving others

I can't stress how important it is to spend at least 10 to 20 percent of your life serving others. There is something special about helping people less fortunate than you. Engaging in meeting the needs of other people helps you exercise your feelings of empathy. It triggers those

> Spend at least 10-20% of your life serving others.

emotions in you that are not self-centered. It forces your ego to humbly recognize its need for compassionate interaction.

James' Story

I remember when James came to my office feeling really depressed, even though he had been on anti-depressants for more than a year. Although he had never attempted suicide, James did engage in risky behaviors that could have cost him his life. After three weeks in therapy, James decided that he would visit his grandmother, who was in a nursing home. When he came to his next session, he mentioned that he had helped her eat and also had pushed her around the park in her wheel chair. His eyes became tearful when he began to express how special it felt for him to be able to assist her and how encouraged he was to see that his life was not as limited as his grandmother's. James thanked God that, even though his situation was less than perfect, it was not nearly as bad as that experienced by some people. James later began gardening and found taking care of plants also helped him stay in touch with himself and keep life into perspective.

6. Take small steps to trusting others

In essence, trust has to do with having confidence in someone or something. Most of the time when we enter into a relationship, we like to feel that we can trust the one we're with. When trust has been violated, it is really hard to get back. And sometimes when we lose our trust in someone in one relationship, it makes it hard to trust anyone else. Broken trust can damage how you behave in relationships for a very long time.

Honesty and reliability are two hallmarks of trust. When someone is honest and reliable you know you can depend on what they say without fear of things falling apart. But trust is also based on experience

> Honesty and reliability are two hallmarks of trust.

– it doesn't just happen. It's a pattern of consistent reliability built over time and, when trust is broken, it is possible to rebuild.

Liars will be liars and they will show themselves to be liars sooner or later; however, be sure you don't treat an honest person like a liar because of your past experience. Sometimes when one person breaks your heart, you put everyone else in the same basket and act as if everyone broke your heart. That's a sure way to miss opportunities for new, healthy relationships.

You shouldn't automatically trust everyone right off the bat, but you should try to trust again. To rebuild your feelings of trust you can begin by taking small risks in giving people the benefit of the doubt. Start with baby steps that don't require much. In some instances, you might have to lower some of your expectations. That's o.k. – just be sure you're not compromising your values.

7. Don't feed your anger with high expectations

Anger is produced when you feel your personal needs are not being met. Anger feeds on the fuel of these unmet expectations and needs. Don't bend the rules to feed your anger's appetite. I often advise people in my anger management program to lower their expectations of others. When

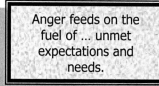

Anger feeds on the fuel of … unmet expectations and needs.

your expectations of others are set too high, there is more opportunity to be disappointed.

Tiger's Story:

In 2009, pro golfer Tiger Woods' private life was made public in a very sordid way when the world learned that the iconic Tiger had several affairs while married to his wife, Elin. The big question for most people was not only should his wife forgive him and stay married to him, but also should the public forgive him and continue to support him as an American role-model. Many people were very angry with him. Their expectations of him were set really high. Children and youths who modeled their life after him were now crushed by the reality that the expectations they had for him were more than he was able to meet. He fell short of meeting the branded mark of human perfection.

When expectations are too high, we often set ourselves up for failure. This does not mean we compromise on helping and encouraging others to meet their goals, but it does mean that we have to make sure those goals are theirs, not ours. It is human nature to have expectations of other people in our lives. But thoughts like "I *know* he will do this," or "I'm sure she won't do that" help to set the stage for failed expectations, which in turn can lead to heartbreak. Then the anger felt by a broken heart feeds off the emotional and psychological energy produced by the failure. The more you think it, the more it is. The more you feel it, the more it becomes. So try to avoid setting expectations in the first place and balance your thoughts and feelings to appropriately accommodate your experiences.

8. A plan for dealing with anger

There are two primary things that you have to be aware of and clearly define in order to develop "healthy anger." The first is what your personal needs are. Identifying your needs in different situations and relationships brings clarity to your expectations and the better they are defined the better off you will be. Remember, we set expectations of others and ourselves to meet our needs. If we had no needs, we would have no expectations.

The second primary thing is to identify how you are going to get those needs met. This can get a bit tricky because sometimes you know what you need, you just don't realize that the way you have tried to get them met in the past wasn't working or was inappropriate.

As I worked on this book, I began to think about how I was always taught that I should do my best to meet the needs of others through serving and helping them. I often did that without even realizing that, in doing so, I was getting some of my own emotional needs met. Whenever you do something to help someone else, there is always a personal underlying need in you that is also being met.

I once asked a father who spent 80% of his life away from home working to make a living for his family, "What do you need from your family?" Surprisingly, this question was harder for him to answer than I expected. He said that he had never thought about what he needed or was getting from them. Instead, he always considered only what they needed him for and what he could do for them. Sometimes we don't even think about what our own needs are and how we are getting them met.

When have you experienced your expectations not being met? What was your response? Now think of the time your heart was broken in the context of your needs and expectations. What was it you needed? How did you expect that need to be met? When the need was unmet, how did the anger that produced in you express itself? No doubt you felt something like your broken heart was being suffocated or torn apart, but what actions resulted from that?

I have seen cases of unforgiveness where a person had lived almost their entire life holding on to anger, not realizing that it was related to expectations and needs. When they learned this process and began making the connections, they were able to identify what their needs were and how they might get those needs met. They were also able to set reasonable expectations for the future that were based on appropriate needs. That was the beginning of resolving their anger and moving on to a life full of hope and a heart unbroken.

THE ANGER DIET
1. Be responsible for your own actions
2. Relax regularly
3. Think positive thoughts
4. Help others
5. Keep your promises

REFRAMING HURTFUL EXPERIENCES

Reframing hurtful experiences is not the same as positive thinking. Positive thinking is the habit of applying positive attributes to all situations. Reframing actually changes the frame (or the lens) you are looking through to see your situation. It's not just simply making a negative thing positive, but it's actually seeing something that looks and feels negative in a completely restructured framework – ultimately improving your visual acuity so you can see things in their true perspective.

Reframing clears things up by ushering you towards the One who stands behind the lens, so you can see the world in the way He intended. In reframing experiences, we look to the ultimate power and source of all allowed experiences – God, because whatever has happened has not in any way, shape or form bypassed His sovereignty. God has an intention and is always available to help you discover the fruit produced from your heartbreak.

Joseph and Job

In the Bible, a man named Joseph helps us to understand this perspective. After all the torment and torture his own brothers put him through, Joseph was still able to forgive them. He attributed their malicious work to the enemy while the end result of all their attempts to destroy him – which actually turned out to his benefit in the long run – he attributed to God. Joseph concluded, "What the enemy meant for evil, God meant for good." Even Satan's plot to have Job curse God never succeeded.

God forever turns your bad circumstances toward His glory. He is going to get the glory out of your situation. The objective for you is to let Him work things out for you. Because He is really good at it! Let Him be the frame or the border for your life portrait.

When a frame is placed around a work of art, it helps to tell the story. That's why artists and photographers take special pains to ensure that a frame matches the picture it is being placed around. A broken frame around a perfectly beautiful picture makes the whole picture look bad – so off it goes to be reframed. In the same way, the pictures in our life need reframing. Broken frames have to be taken off and new frames constructed to accurately show God's intent for our heartbreak. In doing this you will find, like Joseph; "What the devil meant for evil, God meant for Good."

RESTORING SELF-CONFIDENCE

Godly self-confidence can be like a road growing shorter as we grow older. Doesn't it seem like the distances we walked as children to get from one place to the next get so much closer together as we get older? Godly self-confidence works the same way. Confidence in yourself gives you a positive perspective of

> Godly self-confidence promotes Godly character.

what you are able to do. Although sometimes misperceived as being cocky or arrogant, there is a fine line between confidence and arrogance. You *should* feel as though your abilities can make things happen for you and others, and you should put those abilities to work in the most effective ways possible, but it's not your skills or talents alone that make great things happen. Most people have a false perception of their abilities and either lack confidence or are arrogantly over-confident. God wants us to be balanced as we continue to discover how "fearfully and wonderfully" made we are. Godly self-confidence promotes Godly character.

When you are hurt by someone, you may begin to feel worthless or that you can't do anything right. You may even go back to old patterns in your life that led you to think that you are less capable than others in the first place. These are the kinds of things that begin to tear down your self-confidence. The process of forgiveness requires both humility and strength (confidence). It is very difficult for people who lack self-confidence to genuinely forgive others because their view of themselves is so diminished.

The root of the word confidence is "confide," meaning to trust with information. To possess confi-

> To possess confidence is to trust yourself with the truth about who you are.

dence is to trust yourself with the truth about who you are. When you remind yourself you are exactly who God created you to be and you really believe it, you can act on it. You are your own greatest asset to restoring your confidence because it starts with trusting the truth about who God created you to be.

Here are a few other things you can do to build your confidence:

1. Pray for God's help.

2. Dress up – sometimes you should even overdress.

3. Start thinking positive thoughts about yourself.

4. Slow down and speak more clearly.

5. Set small goals and complete them.

6. Smile more often.

7. Do something you have been putting off.

8. Clean up some clutter in your office or home.

9. Get ready! – for something you want to do, and *do it*!!!

Remember that only you can restore your self-confidence and the best way to do that is through *action*. It's not just what you believe or say about yourself, it is what you do that makes the difference.

THE RELATIONSHIP BETWEEN ANGER, GUILT, SHAME AND FEAR

I have identified four negative feelings that may be covering up the real you: **anger, guilt, shame,** and **fear**. Each is like a layer that builds a protective shield over who you are inside. They do this to protect you. It's so paradoxically simple that it often appears complicated. We have already discussed anger extensively; now we'll spend some time discussing guilt, shame and fear. The primary emotion that works to feed your anger and harden your heart is guilt.

Nancy's Story:

Nancy came into my office after her son was stabbed during a fight in the neighborhood. She discussed how she felt so guilty for what had happened to her son – she couldn't stop thinking that it was her fault and that she was not a good parent. Nancy blamed herself for the incident and that lead to her blaming herself for other things surrounding the incident as well. As she talked about her guilt, I realized that this mother did not have a personal life. She had literally dedicated her entire life to her children, who were teenage boys and beginning to get in trouble. Nancy stated that she felt guilty not only about her son being stabbed, but also in almost every area of her life. She felt guilty when she spent money on herself, thinking that the money could be better spent on her children.

Nancy also mentioned that after work she always tried to hurry home. She would feel guilty if she was at work late, because that meant her kids were missing time with her. Some nights she was so exhausted, she would go home and just sit on the couch with little or no interaction with her children. Then she would start feeling guilty about being at home but too tired to engage with them.

One could see Nancy as a dedicated mother who put her children before herself. Yet what's not so obvious, but more important, is the motivation behind the madness. If her self-deprivation were driven by love then it would be good; but if guilt is the motivation, then it's unhealthy.

Finally, she said to me: "I'm guilty about everything. Every time I turn my head, there is something for me to feel guilty about. I wish I could be free to be me!"

We began to discuss her guilt in the context of grief. Grief is the result of loss (when something you hope to have happen, does not). People grieve the death of a loved one because they hoped that person would have lived. When they grieve a broken relationship, they hoped that it would have lasted. Somewhere deep in all of us is the hope that things will work out the way we want them to. Anything that diminishes our hope can cause grief. It's not just the loss that hurts; not being able to realize what we hoped for causes the most pain.

Guilt has to do with you blaming yourself for something that happened. Even if it was not your fault, you still find a way to feel responsible. Somehow you decide the crime that was committed has to have a suspect and it has to be you. You convince yourself that you are to blame for everything that goes wrong and give yourself little credit for things you've done right. Somewhere along the line you lost something, and you have been blaming yourself for it. Your conclusion: "It's all my fault."

That's where Nancy was, and in counseling she realized quickly that she needed to continue moving through the grief process. Feeling guilty was part of it, but it was not the whole of it. It was a beginning, but was truly not the end.

As we began to deeply explore her guilt in the context of grief, we learned that Nancy felt she was losing the opportunity to prove to herself that she was different than her mother. Nancy disclosed that she set a lifetime goal of never being like her mother, who was a recovering drug addict and did not take very good care of her children. Nancy was embarrassed by her mother. She thought she would be there for her own boys every time they needed her. She wanted to be the mother to her children that she didn't have growing up.

But now Nancy realized how similar to her mother she really was. As a matter of fact, for the first time ever in her life, she confessed that she had been using marijuana on a regular basis for years. Internally she was grieving the loss of her ambition to be different than her mother while at the same time feeling guilty about her drug use at a massive level. This guilt was playing itself out in every aspect of her life.

Eventually Nancy's guilt would turn to anger, her anger would lead to her shame, and shame would make her fearful of ever trying to change. She would become crippled by fear and resistant to dealing with the internal issues and feelings she had inside.

We often think fear exists by itself. We think that, if we defeat it, then we will be able to accomplish the things we desire. In reality, fear is generated by so many other emotions. Nancy had to deal with grief, guilt and shame as well as fear because guilt and shame were the energy in her fear tank.

> Who you are is never determined by what you have been through; rather, it is how well you understand what you have been through that helps to improve who you are becoming.

Every incident of your life is connected to a feeling,

and incidents and feelings start to cover up who you really are. That's why it's important to deal with these issues so that you can free yourself from their bondage. You deserve to be free. Who you are is never determined by what you have been through; rather, it is how well you understand what you have been through that helps to improve who you are becoming.

Sarah's Story:

In my early years as a Christian therapist, I recall working with another woman who was in a similar situation. When Sarah came to see me, she had one question. She sat back in her chair, looked me in the eyes and said, "Please don't tell me what Jesus can do for me, I already know that. I need something I can put my hands on."

Like a good counselor, impressed by her strong religious conviction but confused about what she meant, I remained silent for a moment, and then eventually responded by saying, "Can you tell me more about what you mean?"

As she continued to talk, Sarah covered her face with both hands and began to weep. Her make-up ran down her face and her Sunday-church-service presentation fell away. After every sob, she gasped for air only to further condemn herself. "I don't love myself ... I fool people with my religious visage ... I can't explain where my pain is ..." She made these statements between teardrops. Eventually Sarah removed her hands from her face and began to hold herself in her desperate need for help. Then she wiped another tear and lifted her head, as if to say she would be O.K. But life would not allow her to deceive herself this time, and she began to cry again and said, "I need to know who I am. What does it mean to be a woman?"

Most females don't identify themselves as women until their late twenties and early thirties, and some never think about it. When asked what defines a woman, they normally repeat what they have been taught by their parents, grandparents, and mentors. Responses such as taking care of their family and doing for others seem to make the top ten list every time. But, the essence of womanhood is more than the things she does. It is the discovery of who she is and how this impacts her life. Powders, perfumes and self-pampering often cover up "who she is" – the part of her that has lived in the dark shadows of her soul, shyly peeking out every once in a while, only to retreat back inside.

Even though she may have been taught the do's and don'ts of life by older women, Sarah's real training happened in her own mind and through her own experiences. Many of her memories were too painful, disappointing and heartbreaking to share with anyone, so she relied on herself to make difficult decisions and to make sense of difficult events. She had painful secrets that she thought no one else could possibly understand.

Things would be different if life were as perfect as she made it up in her imagination during childhood. When Sarah was little, she created a perfect world with her baby dolls, and her make believe castles. The dolls only "felt" what she wanted them to feel. They only "spoke" what she wanted spoken. When they cried, she could ask why and answer the question herself.

But what does a child do when her baby dolls don't stop crying? What does she do when their pain doesn't seem to end? The young girl begins to see the realities of life, and she struggles with losing control of a perfect world. In an attempt to maintain stability, part of her is pushed away into a corner and eventually left behind. The part of her she needs the most is left to live in the dark. The part of her that holds her dreams, goals and purpose in life is left to hide its face forever – or at least until she begins the work of un-breaking her heart.

EXERCISES

Forgiveness Phase III – Redemption
Assignment 1:

Make a list of your five primary needs and tell how you get those needs met. Use the space below or another sheet of paper to complete the assignment:

My five primary (personal) needs and how I get them met:

1. _____

2. _____

3. _____

4. _____

5. _____

Now list the expectations these needs placed on you and others:

1. _____

2. _____

3. _____

4. _____

5. _____

Forgiveness Phase III – Redemption
Assignment 2:

In the following section, match an activating event in your life to a reaction and a motivating belief:

ACTIVATING EVENT	REACTION	MOTIVATING BELIEF
(He cheated on me)	(I hit him)	(He doesn't love me)

1. _____

2. _____

3. _____

4. _____

5. _____

Forgiveness PHASE III – Redemption
Assignment 3:

List five of your noticeable signs of anger below. The opposite of anger is love. Resolving anger will always restore a genuine love and concern for people. So next to your list of anger signs (in the first column), list their opposite under the love column:

ANGER SIGNS *OPPOSITE* **LOVE SIGNS**

1. _____   _____

2. _____   _____

3. _____   _____

4. _____   _____

Forgiveness PHASE III – Redemption
Assignment 4:

The objective of this exercise is to move your mind and emotions from anger to love. Read the following scriptures. In the adjacent space, write down what you will do to become better in each area.

1 Corinthians 13:4-8

[4]Love is patient　　　　　　_____

Love is kind　　　　　　_____

It does not envy　　　　　　_____

It does not boast　　　　　　_____

It is not proud　　　　　　_____

[5]It is not rude　　　　　　_____

It is not self-seeking　　　　　　_____

It is not easily angered _____

It keeps no record of wrongs _____

[6]*Love does not delight in evil* _____

But rejoices with the truth _____

[7]*It always protects* _____

Always trusts _____

Always hopes _____

Always perseveres _____

To love means loving the unlovable. To forgive means pardoning the unpardonable. Faith means believing the unbelievable. Hope means hoping when everything seems hopeless. ~ Gilbert K. Chesterson

CHAPTER 9

THE RECOVERY ROOM

A POST-OP TO-DO LIST FOR MENDING A BROKEN HEART

A broken heart often produces feelings of depression that show themselves in many different ways. That's why it's important for you to do the following when you are recovering from a broken heart:

1. Recognize the fact that it is not you who is dying, but it is simply love that is giving up. Because love is so much a part of you, it feels like your own personal life is ending. But the fact of the matter is that in order for love to survive, first you must survive. You have to keep things into perspective.

2. Take care of your physical health by eating an adequate diet. Sometimes you may not feel like eating, even though you know you need to. A broken heart will sometimes make your body think that it is not hungry, or that it doesn't need to eat. You have to be smarter

than your broken heart and remember that food is a necessity and, even if you don't feel like eating, you have to eat to survive.

Or sometimes you want to give in to a craving for comfort food – ice cream, chocolate, pasta or pizza – even though putting on weight is not in your best interests. Your broken heart makes your body feel that it needs to eat constantly to help it feel better; but no amount of food can fill the hole in your heart. You know that overeating can be just as detrimental as not eating enough, so don't over-eat either.

Remember to keep a well-balanced diet and have a friend or family member help monitor your eating habits to ensure that you are on track.

3. Stay involved in activities that kept you busy previously and continue to do things that you once enjoyed doing. Stay connected with your friends and family. A broken heart will make you feel like you need to isolate yourself. It will make you think that no one wants to hear about your problems.

   Remember that people love and care about you, and they want to be around you. They are there to help you and they are on your side. God created you for those friendships. Force yourself to stay involved.

4. Guard your heart from negative thoughts. One of the gifts God gave you is your ability to counter negative thinking about yourself. For example, if you feel like you can't do anything, and you feel hopeless and helpless,

you can counter that with positive self-talk: *(I can do all things through Christ who gives me strength. – Philippians 4:13)*. Meditate and repeat that to yourself, but don't stop there. The enemy (depression, despondency) has a tendency to try to use broken hearts to play mind games on you, so arm yourself with positive thoughts.

5. Take action. When you say you can do all things through Christ, who strengthens you, you have to act on that. You have to literally get up and do something.

6. Your broken heart may want to sleep all the time, but you know it's time to get up, so get up! An adequate amount of sleep is necessary for a healthy life, but too little or too much sleep can cause problems.

7. Seek help. Problems concentrating, excessive irritability, body aches, pains and lack of energy may also result from the depression caused by a broken heart.

   Remember, when things are too overwhelming and you can't seem to get over these feelings, seek professional help. You may want to contact a hospital, psychiatrist, psychologist, counselor or family doctor. Don't delay. There is no weakness in looking for guidance from another person. It is better to have this kind of help to get through these feelings than to try to do it alone.

   Especially if you experience thoughts or feelings of suicide, be sure to seek help and tell someone. The objective is to live, and you can't do that by bottling things up and not letting others know how you are feeling. So – even if you feel others are not listening – talk! Talk! *Talk!*

Read this to-do list every day until you know it by heart. You *will* get through this and love will live again, but it takes time and effort.

*Occasionally in life there are those moments of unutterable fulfillment,
which cannot be completely explained by those symbols called words.
Their meanings can only be articulated by the inaudible language of
the heart. ~ Martin Luther King, Jr.*

CHAPTER 10

PHASE IV: REVEALING

*THE HEALING JOURNEY – ALL THINGS WORKING
TOGETHER FOR GOOD*

The **REVEALING PHASE is the fourth phase of forgiveness.** You are now taking your first steps on the road to recovery from open-heart surgery. This is the phase that begins to balance the realities of life. Its ultimate objective is to help you rebuild your experience. You landed in the Emergency Room and received the diagnosis of a broken heart in Phase I; you were given a prognosis in Phase II and in Phase III you came through the surgery to cut out your anger. Now, as God's truth about the circumstances leading to your broken heart is gradually unveiled to you through prayer and introspection during the Revealing Phase, you will redefine and build perspective, decrease the intensity of negative feelings, change your attitude and re-establish the hope necessary for you to live in love again.

Revealing is also the fourth stage of a broken heart, as listed in Chapter 3. Further along in this chapter, you'll see how two more of my clients, Tambra and Carlton, each moved through the Revealing Stage of their broken hearts.

Think about this for a second: the person who offended you did it, if not totally, then at least partly because of their own deep hurt and suffering due to things that happened to them in their past. Their life condition set the stage for what they did to you, just as your life condition sets the stage for how you interact with other people. When you understand that, you will begin to see how fragile humanity really is and how deeply wounded most people are. This is not to say that you go around hurting people the way they did you, but you acknowledge how we are all influenced by outside forces and how the circumstances of our personal lives prompt us to act in certain ways. This does not justify wrong behavior, but does lend credibility to the saying, "hurt people, hurt people."

> [T]he person who offended you did it ... because of their own deep hurt and suffering...

But why should you feel sorry for the person who betrayed you? Why should you begin to rebuild your perspective in a way that seems to favor them, when you were the one who was wronged? First of all, because you want to deal with the truth. Truth is really what frees you to a clear conscience and an unbroken heart. As vague a concept as truth may be for many, it has got to become crystallized for you.

It was in the light of this paradigm shift that I was able to understand how a woman who had been beaten, raped and buried alive could dig herself out of the ground and, ten years later while in therapy, begin to feel deeply sorry for the people who did that to her. She once said, "I know whatever prompted them to do that to me must be much more painful for them than it was for me." Her point was that it's got to be hard to live with the pain of evil intentions and acts, whether you are aware of them or not.

People who hurt you take things from you that only time can replace. One of the main things they take from you is your creativity. When someone violates you to the point of leaving you with bitterness and anger in your heart, they rob you of being the fluid and genuinely creative person God created you to be. Unforgiveness prevents that creativity from being restored to you.

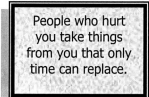

People who hurt you take things from you that only time can replace.

In the Revealing Phase, you move from being a victim to becoming a survivor. There is a thin line between the two. A victim is helpless and at the will of the wrongdoer. A survivor is hopeful and at the will of their own self-determination. The victim is defined by what was done to them (keeping the act in the present). A survivor puts the act behind them (in the past) and moves forward. Victory is achieved primarily because you survived an incident that could have destroyed you. You were a victim of the act (not the person) and you survived.

The objective in weighing the significance of the person who hurt you against the hurtful act they committed is to gain a new empathy for your offender that encourages you to want to see them get help so they won't do to others what they did to you. Looking at the situation through this new perspective actually stretches your imagination and brings you back in touch with your own creativity.

Do you know that feeling when you are at your best; when you are "in the zone" and you are confident in your own gifting and ability? When you know your own competencies and are able to both articulate them and put them to use? That's your creative spirit at work. Everyone deserves to live at that level. As you get back to your creative place, you will find you are able to make the kind of decisions that are not based on anger, but rather on wisdom and truth, because good creative decisions come from good creative places.

As I was watching my daughter play with her baby dolls one day several years ago, I began to reflect on the many children I had worked with using their toys as therapeutic aids. I was often surprised at how quickly innocent amusement – playing at school teacher, for instance – could turn to aggressive behavior as they tried to resolve the inner conflicts and pain caused by abuse or other traumatic events. They attempted to put their emotional world back together through play. The question was, would these children who were trying to resolve dysfunction ever be able to return to the pure innocence of simply playing with their toys?

You may wish life could always be happy and that bad things would never happen. But they do, and the best you can do is make the effort to get back to how you felt mentally and emotionally prior to that time. Forgiveness helps you to move to the place where your thoughts are not filtered through fear but through love, not in complaining but in gratitude, not in anxiety but in peace and not in anger but in pardon.

> Forgiveness helps you to move to the place where your thoughts are not filtered through fear but through love, not in complaining but in gratitude, not in anxiety but in peace and not in anger but in pardon.

PURPOSE AND PERSPECTIVE

If your perspective is negative and unclear, your purpose will always be negative and unclear. I often say that I don't know why something happened, only God knows that, but I can look at the circumstances and build perspective around that. I can have a positive

> If your perspective is negative and unclear then your purpose will always be negative and unclear.

effect on others rather than a negative one. Sometimes you may feel like you have to impress others for them to accept you, or at least they have to see that you are strong and brave. You are quick to jump to premature facets of forgiveness and act like you are OK when you're really not.

One of the perspectives that needs to change during this stage is how you see the state that you are in. You made it through what happened and the mere fact that you are able to reflect back on it and hurt about it is evidence that you have made it. You may still be hurting, angry or resentful, but the situation is over and you are no longer helpless victim; you're a survivor. You are healing.

The mistake some people make is judging the state they are in by how they feel. Since the feeling is the same as it was when the event happened ("I still feel so horrified about what happened"), they believe that the state is the same ("I just can't live like normal people ever again; this is always going to haunt me"). They operate from the perspective of still being in the situation because it still feels like they are. In the chapter on Phase I of forgiveness, the Realization Phase, we used the metaphor of a rainstorm and the difference between being *in* the storm and just being wet *from* the storm. Simply because you are still wet doesn't mean it's still raining.

In the Realization Phase you took those first steps to help you accept the experience of the storm. Now it is time to rebuild your perspective of reality and know that you are truly out of that bad situation. Wet, but out of the rain and it's time to dry off. These realizations will change the rest of your life.

You've heard the analogy that "the glass is either half empty or half full." If you see the glass as half empty, you may feel like things are going badly. If you see it as half full, you may feel more enthusiastic about the situation. These two familiar options lend themselves to a dependence on how the water in the glass is measured. Looking at how much water you have available forces you to calculate or categorize your situation. While it helps to know when the cup seems half full because you are seeing things from a positive perspective, that's just part of thinking positive.

I propose a *third* option that simply states, "I have water!" Whether you see your glass as half empty or half full doesn't change the amount of water you have. With the third option, the question becomes more about *what* you see and how what you see supersedes *how* you see it. Because what you see determines where you choose to go from here – your future path.

WHY ME?

You are left to tell the story, but why? Regardless of how horrible the memories and how dreadful the mood, you survived! So many people couldn't live with the same thing happening to them, so why you? Why have you survived? Why have you been left and empowered to tell your story? Why has God kept you?

This is a question that only you can answer, and the answer will gradually be revealed to you – maybe a just little at a time – as you progress on your healing path. Whatever God has in His mind for you, you must accomplish it. Yes, it may be a little difficult, and you might move towards it a little more slowly than others, but you didn't survive *that* to die in *this*. You were on the table and the surgery was performed; now – on your way to victory!

You need to rebuild your strength and you'll have to do it in a scheduled and organized way.

As you reconstruct your life and search for the strength to forgive, you may begin to feel empathetic towards your offender. This comes from the realization that, from a biblical perspective, all have sinned and fallen short of the glory of God *(Romans 3:23)*. Yet, unforgiving thoughts of not letting your abuser get away with what they did to you may come to mind. At first forgiveness may feel as though you are letting them take advantage of you – *again!* Keep the perspective straight and remind yourself: that battle is not yours to fight in the first place. They are not getting over on *you*; their accountability is to God, and they can't get over on Him – He will deal with them. I've actually seen circumstances where God dispensed his justice through the very people the culprit offended – and this may be the case for you.

An example was a young lady who told her stepfather that she forgave him for the abuse she had experienced from his hands during her childhood. He literally felt so guilty because of her exposure of the abuse that he could not handle it alone and called for God to help him. He later committed himself to the Lord and spent the rest of his life trying to repair the relationships he so deeply damaged.

THE BALANCING FACTOR

Have you ever made a mistake? Ever done something that you regretted? Have you ever hurt anyone intentionally or unintentionally? Maybe you haven't done anything even close to what happened to hurt you, but we've all done something that hurt another person or things we are not necessarily proud of. We've all needed to be forgiven before by someone, for something. I say this with confidence because none of us are perfect. That doesn't give us permission to do wrong, nor does it justify the wrong done to you, but it is true. This phase of forgiveness takes an authentic look at our own faults to help us understand the limitations of people and the limitlessness of God. I mentioned earlier in the book that every one of us acts out of our own circumstances, including you.

Most people make the mistake of trying to get to the Revealing Phase too early in the process. But this chapter is the fourth phase of the process and is placed towards the end of the book because, by the time you have worked through all the previous phases, you are more prepared for this kind of thinking. This phase cannot be undertaken by itself. If you skipped over all the rest of the book to read this chapter, you'll probably put the book down and write to me with a lot of questions. If you are not ready to do the work of this chapter, please simply go back to other phases of forgiveness and continue to work through some of the issues there. You will probably find the answer to your questions.

Some pastors and pastoral counselors make the mistake of

> Life works in stages. Don't put your emotional self ahead of where you really are.

pushing people to this phase before they are ready, which normally causes more guilt and does more harm than good. In many ways, it re-victimizes the victim, so you have to be careful. Some people take years to get to this level, while others may take only weeks. The important thing is that you work through all the issues related to anger before you get here, because trying to work this phase without working through the anger will only make you angrier. Life works in stages. Don't put your emotional self ahead of where you really are.

REORGANIZING THINGS AROUND GOD'S TRUTH

I mentioned in an earlier chapter that biblical forgiveness is both a principle and a process. Focusing on the principle of forgiveness without dealing with the process ignores the human and emotional aspects of forgiveness; and focusing on the process while ignoring the principle ignores its spiritual and supernatural aspects. Forgiveness has to be done in both Spirit and in truth (honestly). In order to clearly understand forgiveness, we obviously need a model and I like to use the story of forgiveness from the Bible.

I mentioned previously that the essence of forgiveness is love and, since God is love, He is the model by which this philosophy of forgiveness is understood. With love comes forgiveness and with forgiveness comes love. The two are interchangeable – one and the same. One cannot exist without the other. When love came to the earth, forgiveness came with it.

> When love came to the earth, forgiveness came with it.

Both love and forgiveness are gifts that God actually gave to everyone. The Bible is a love story of how God forgave the people He created to worship Him. There is no more significant example than the forgiveness God gave us through Jesus Christ.

Yes, the emotional and psychological elements of your experience are real and need to be dealt with, but God still has to move in and begin to heal you for that to happen. Amazingly, His story of love for you is laid out in a fashion of forgiveness similar to the way this book is written for you. God Himself moved His Wrath to Love in Jesus Christ and, in doing this, He opened the opportunity for us to be forgiven. Let me show you how moving *your* progression from anger to love is the method so essential for your divine healing. If you want to really get it right, then get it from the One who had it right in the first place – God. Remember, the anger produced from the heartbreak has to be completely resolved through forgiveness before you can begin that a new and better life that you are hoping for and that *is* before you.

Now let's take a look at the principle of biblical forgiveness and see how this process is evident in God's forgiveness of us.

UNDERSTANDING GOD'S FORGIVENESS

When God created Adam and Eve, He created them for His glory. They were to worship Him and be in His presence all the time. But one day they disobeyed God and ate the fruit of the forbidden tree. They became totally separated from God and, expelled from Eden, began to experience a life of struggle and tragedy. Eventually, their son Cain killed his brother Abel and, from that point on, God's people would turn their backs on Him. You'll find many references to scriptures that illustrate God's anger (wrath) towards His people because of their sins and disobedience.

Well, God would not let His anger just fester forever because He loved His people so much, so He chose to resolve it. God, who is just, demonstrated His love through His precise and just act of sacrifice. It was humanity that sinned against Him, so humanity would have to pay the debt. But here is an apparent paradox: everything humans have – and could ever pay back – came first from God, so humanity could never by themselves pay the debt back, because they had nothing that God hadn't given them. Yet, because the debt was legitimately owed, it had to be paid back – it could not be written off.

The solution was left to someone who was both God and man: Jesus Christ. As God, He could make the payment – because He owned everything He had. And as man, He could satisfy justice – because man committed the crime. In all of this, God was pleased to sacrifice His only Son to die for the sins of the world. His wrath was resolved in the act of sacrificial service for the sins of humanity. Our hope of reconciliation and a blessed life together with God, was realized only after anger (wrath) had been resolved. Our condition didn't prompt God to abandon and forget about us, but rather to love us and to want the best for us.

As you probably are already thinking, forgiveness of sin didn't come easily, but came through great sacrifice. Forgiveness *never* comes easily; more often than not, it forces us to make some of the toughest choices life has to offer. But when we allow it to work, our lives are changed forever.

> Forgiveness *never* comes easily; more often than not, it forces us to make some of the toughest choices life has to offer.

This was only a summary of how God's anger towards us was resolved in Jesus Christ and how all hope was found for us in that same act of sacrifice. Below is a list of Bible scriptures that will guide you through the world's greatest love story – the resolution of God's anger and the realization of our hope through the act of His forgiveness. You may choose to keep a journal as you read through these scriptures.

Forgiveness through Jesus Christ is available to everyone:

Psalm 51:1-17

1 John 1:5-10

Romans 10:5-13

Psalm 32:1-11

Romans 8:31-39

Romans 3:21-26

New life in Christ allows us to live in the freedom and hope of God's original plan for life:

Romans 6:1-14

Matthew 20:20-28

Ephesians 4:17-32

Galatians 5:16-26

1 John 4:7-21

Romans 12:1-21

We are all in need of God's forgiveness because of sin; we were all separated from God because of sin:

Isaiah 59:1-15
Romans 3:9-20
Romans 5:12-21
Romans 7:14-25

God loves us and, despite our sins, He always wants to form a close relationship with us:

Exodus 19:3-8
Jeremiah 31:31-34
Isaiah 54:1-10
1 Peter 1:1-10
1 John 3:1-10

God's love is fully expressed by His sending Jesus Christ to us:

Colossians 1:15-23
Romans 5:1-11
1 Peter 2:10-25
John 3:1-21
2 Timothy 1:3-10
Ephesians 2:1-10

WHO'S GOING TO DEFEND YOU?

It is no mystery that you want to get back at the person who hurt you. Anger will always want to defend itself with your help. Your body was designed to protect itself and it *will* defend itself even without your consent because that is what it does. God created you in such a way that, when you are violated or placed in

> Anger will always want to defend itself with your help.

any risky or dangerous situation, your body figures out how to safeguard itself. It fights against any harm done to it or it flees to protect itself. It's a natural phenomenon.

Protecting yourself is so much a natural part of who you are that when you cut yourself, before any ointment is applied, before any bandages are placed on the wound, the white blood cells have already identified the point of attack and swarmed over to begin the natural healing process at the site of the wound. You don't have to tell your body to do that; it does it automatically because it is designed to care for itself *(After all, no one ever hated his own body, but he feeds and cares for it, just as Christ does the church – Ephesians 5:29).*

The body can do extraordinary things in an effort to protect you from pain. Many clients in treatment for sexual abuse or severe repeated trauma have explained episodes of disassociation where they literally experienced themselves watching the abuse happen from a corner in the room while it was taking place. They were able to evade the pain and feelings connected with the abuse by removing themselves emotionally from their physical body, so that they were protected from the incident.

The same is true when your heart has been broken. Anger forms as a natural response to the situation and begins to stimulate thoughts and other emotions that encourage you to defend yourself. As a plan, vengeance harbors in your heart and you begin to think about how unfair life is, or you ask why God allowed this to happen to you or why you always get the short end of the stick. God's response is, "Vengeance is mine."

You might expect God's vengeance would destroy the person who hurt you. Instead, you see God giving His grace to that person who so damaged you – and it just doesn't seem fair! God's vengeance is given in love and sacrifice and He offers this grace to your perpetrator even after what that person did to you. You feel frustrated because it doesn't seem like justice, but it *is* God. If God is willing to forgive your perpetrator, maybe you should give it a try as well.

> If God is willing to forgive your perpetrator, maybe you should give it a try

Tambra's Story:

I'll never forget working with Tambra, who was in a very abusive relationship. One night her boyfriend actually tried to choke her to death and later put a gun to her head and threatened to kill her in front of her daughter. After she pleaded for her life in fear, he turned the gun on himself and stated, "No, it's not you that needs to die. It's me. I am the bad guy. Look what I've done to you."

Tambra frantically began to beg him not to kill himself. She grabbed the gun and tried to pull it away from him. With tears and fear, she wrapped her arms around him and held him in pity, hoping that things would change. He put the gun down, but Tambra's boyfriend never changed and one day Tambra got the courage to leave.

After being separated from him for about two years, Tambra was diagnosed with cancer and began to wonder how his life could be going so well and hers be so difficult. Sometimes it seems like the person who causes the pain, gets off easier than the one that suffers the pain. Sometimes it looks like God does nothing to people who hurt you and that's when you feel you've got to handle things yourself. Even if you don't actually do anything to that hurtful person, you at least keep hoping that God will punish them for what they did to you.

But finally you learn that God is able to forgive their wrong, and you have to deal with that reality. You realize that God has the power of love that can turn their life around. You consider that, just as He saved you, He can save them. Just as He rescued you, He can also rescue them. And He does. Ponder that for a moment: God doesn't always respond to our pain by inflicting pain on those who hurt us.

So the real question is not whether or not God is on our side, but rather *are we on God's side*? Even if that means we are now on the side of forgiving our offender.

> [T]he real question is not whether or not God is on our side, but rather *are we on God's side*?

FULLY DEPENDING ON GOD

Broken hearts need God. A broken heart understands the need for emergency surgery, and it also understands its treating practitioner (God). It knows that there is a Balm in Gilead, a lifter of heavy burdens and a safe refuge for its pain. God calls the broken-hearted to Himself first *(Come to me, all you who are weary and burdened, and I will give you rest. ~ Matthew 11:28).* Those who have labored to fill the emptiness in their heart, come to Him for rest and healing.

One way to think of forgiveness is that it has to do with "giving as before" *(FOR / GIVE)*, but now with the added component of your new-found wisdom. You will need the Great Physician to help you adopt His perspective of giving as you gave before, *with wisdom.* God loved you and wanted you to know how much He loved you long before you needed to forgive that person who offended you. Even in the midst of your heartbreak, He cared for you.

Your broken heart needs safety. It needs a place to just simply be. It needs somewhere beyond logical understanding because it is getting ready to do something that is far beyond logical reasoning – it's getting ready to forgive. It needs the Creator of forgiveness to give His creation (you and your broken heart) the power to forgive. Your broken heart needs someone to comfort and strengthen it toward a deeper understanding of the situation. It needs someone who can last long and wait well. It needs God and a broken heart fully depends on God to push you through the open-heart surgery and heal you. Its full weight is resting on Him; if He moves away, it falls. It's up to God and only He can get the broken-hearted through this trouble to the fully healthy life ahead.

> [You] need the Creator of forgiveness to give His creation ... the power to forgive.

LEVELING THE PLAYING FIELD

Have you ever wished that something in your past had never happened or that you had made a different decision that maybe would have prevented things from happening the way they did? Everyone looks back sometimes and regrets things. But in reality, you can't change what happened. You can only find a new way to go on with your life. Leveling the playing field will help you to get over regret and get on with your life.

Carlton's Story:

I have helped several troubled couples learn this basic principle of life: that most of the things you accuse your partner of, you are either guilty of yourself, or you have at least thought about it. A husband once accused his wife of talking too much to people at work about her personal life. Carlton was concerned that she was being too intimate with certain people on the job.

As we continued to talk, however, he confessed that he had been having conversations about some of the same things with people on the internet. When Carlton disclosed this, his defense was that he would never see these people in person. The ultimate therapeutic question became, "What's the difference?" Carlton

> [M]ost of the things you accuse your partner of, you are either guilty of yourself, or you have at least thought about it.

realized that there was none. He was guilty of the same thing of which he was accusing his wife.

Why do people do that? Why do people act like they can do no wrong but always feel free to point out *your* shortcomings? Okay, not nice – but haven't you done the same thing before as well? That's why I tell people to be careful about saying, "I would never do that!" Learn to be humble enough to know that you are capable of anything, and you need help to keep from doing or saying things you will regret for the rest of your life. There is not one person on Earth who is good all the time *(As it is written: "There is no one righteous, not even one". – Romans 3:10)* and one of the ways to keep yourself grounded in this reality is to forgive people for their acts against you.

The person who offended you is God's creation. The same God who created you and is giving you the power to forgive is the God who created your abuser. Even if that individual is not Christian, they were still created by God and deserve the opportunity to be forgiven. Bearing and accepting the pain that your offender caused and being empathetic towards that person seems a little crazy sometimes, and it also seems unfair. But life is not fair, it just *is*. Your strength to bear and accept the pain that this person caused will be a testimony to them that you are strong in apparent weakness.

Most people expect you to fight best when you are well prepared and to play well when you are well practiced, but here is one of those incidents where you win the battle even while hurting. The moral gift of showing empathy towards your offender and doing good to the one who hurt you will shine brightly as a reflection of the God you serve. Even if this situation seems too big and painful to forgive, you should still give it a try.

Or you could choose to start by forgiving lesser offenses in your life and then work your way up gradually to forgiving "the big one." Ultimately, you have to get to that point because, when you do, you will mentally and spiritually "buy yourself back" and will be able to apply new meaning and perspectives to your interpretation of life which will change you and the people around you.

Habits are created by doing the same thing over and over. Producing *bad* habits is all too easy. Instead, you can choose to create a habit of forgiveness by repeating it over and over again. It may feel awkward at first, but practice forgiveness regularly in all different situations and you will become familiar with the good feeling it produces. The more you do it, the less foreign it will be to you. Your body will begin to respond to it as a natural part of its chemistry, rather than some strange act, as you continue to practice it. That's what Jesus meant when he said to forgive "seventy-seven times." *(Then Peter came to Jesus and asked, "Lord, how many times shall I forgive my brother when he sins against me? Up to seven times?" Jesus answered, "I tell you, not seven times, but seventy-seven times."– Matthew 18:21-22)* Keep doing it and you will become a master of forgiveness.

GOD'S FORGIVENESS REVEALS YOUR PROMISING FUTURE

In reality, people are responsible to God, but they don't have to conform to our expectations. The line of expectation you placed on the incident marks a broken heart – someone did what you *didn't* expect him or her to do. As you take responsibility for establishing the expectation, you'll see that you anticipated that the other person would have been fully able to meet it. Now that they have broken your heart, it is clear that they could not satisfy the expectation. Thank God you have boundaries, limits and expectations; but be sorry for them, since they could not live up to those expectations. No doubt, they need help – not necessarily from you but, at the least, from God.

And God can help them. He wants them to turn their life around as so many have done with His help. God doesn't have a problem with them. He has a problem with their behavior, but not with them. You have to try to see your abuser through the same lens. It is healthy to be able to accept people and reject destructive behavior. All healthy relationships have boundaries and when those boundaries are violated, we should begin reestablishing them by accepting that people make mistakes while rejecting the mistakes they make. My grandmother always called it "loving the sinner, but hating the sin."

I remember working with a family where a child had been removed from the home because her stepfather had sexually abused her. I had been working with the child in play therapy for about six months while the stepfather was getting treatment as a sex offender. The family was in the process of reuniting after being separated by the state system for four years. The daughter felt that she was ready to confront her stepfather about the abuse he caused her.

My first interview with the stepfather was very difficult. During the interview he explained in detail the things that he had done to his stepdaughter and the pain he felt he caused her. He was tearful and very remorseful. Since I had been treating the stepdaughter for some time, a big part of me wanted to defend her. I was angry with the man and thought to myself, "So you think that treatment, crying and God can fix the things you did?"

Then I thought again: "Yes, they can!"

Still, I was between a rock and a hard place defending a hurt and saddened child from abuse and while also helping to restore a perpetrator to life again. "Are some things too bad to let go?" I asked myself. Then I remembered that humanity is so fragile and so capable of harm. Anybody can do anything at any time. Without God, everything bad is possible. Left only to their own devices and their own minds, lacking a spiritual and moral anchor, people are bound to do whatever occurs to them without caring about consequences.

But I know God can heal and empower the victim and deliver the perpetrator and that is the perspective from which I continued to work with this family. The child would never forget what happened, but she could forgive what happened. Forgiveness doesn't have amnesia; it remembers everything. But it can remember in new ways that promote hopeful perspectives for the future – pressing towards the mark of the high calling in Christ Jesus. Life was never about leaving your past; it is about leading your past into your future.

> Forgiveness doesn't have amnesia.

DESENSITIZING EMOTIONS

The main way to desensitize your negative emotions is to engage in positive experiences. You must begin creating new experiences for yourself. For example, a bad relationship that didn't work out and that may have left you with a broken heart should not stop you from trying a new relationship. Trust that engagement in new positive experiences can help you heal from old negative ones. This is not to say that you should just jump into another relationship, but that you should at least consider the possibility that a good relationship could still be in the works for you. There is a point in everyone's life when they dream enthusiastically of the possibilities life can bring them and the impact they can make on the world. But when life throws you a curve, it's easy to forget your dream and live only with your hurtful memories. Engaging in positive experiences will help to create new happy memories and promote new perspectives and dreams in your life.

> The main way to desensitize your negative emotions is to engage in positive experiences.

THE ATTITUDE ADJUSTMENT

As you work through these issues and resolve your anger while reframing your life around God's truth, you will find that your attitude is being impacted by the freedom you're discovering as a result of the spiritual and emotional work you are doing in forgiving your offender. You may not necessarily recognize it right away because most people are not very familiar with what constitutes attitude and are not aware of changes in their attitude. As you might expect, the Attitude Chamber of your heart is where attitudes originate. Although we use the term "attitude" all the time, we still don't have a clear perspective on what it is or how it works.

What do we mean when we say he or she has a "bad attitude?" How do you get attitudes and what can you do to change attitudes? Well, attitudes are a combination of information, thoughts and feelings around a subject, especially about a particular person or group of people. We are not born with certain attitudes; they are learned as we grow and experience situations in our life. They may be handed down by our parents, picked up from our schoolmates, or adopted from things we have read or heard in the media. But they are always open to new ideas and information, so even if we acquired them a long time ago, we can change them now. That's right – attitudes can be changed. You don't have to keep a bad attitude.

> That's right – attitudes can be changed.

Let's say you're in a relationship with someone and that person lies and cheats on you. You may have given all your heart to that person and they in turn disrespected and violated you by not telling the truth and cheating. Quite naturally, you are going to develop an attitude, not only towards that person, but also towards other people like them. For example, you may think that all men are dogs and no man can be faithful because of your experience with a few men who were like that. Or a man may think that no woman can be trusted after his wife of ten years cheats on him. The feeling you have about them is coupled with the thoughts of your past experience and produces a particular attitude towards them and people like them.

Jane and Mark's Story:

I will never forget Jane, a client who came into counseling because her heart was broken by difficulties she was having in her relationship. Jane felt as though her husband, Mark, was neglecting her and no longer paid her any attention. There were specific things she mentioned that he did to make her feel this way, such as not complimenting her on the way she looked or the things she wore. She said she got more compliments from the outside world than she did in her own home. In response to the way Mark treated her, she stated that she had developed a terrible attitude towards him and was beginning to feel as though she was tired of being married to him. Obviously, love had stopped working in the Attitude Chamber. It had gotten clogged up and was causing major problems for her. As she continued to explain how she felt and thought about things, she made a big sigh and said, "God, my heart is hurting."

Jane mentioned that there was a point in the marriage when her husband asked for some "space." He felt as though they were just always in each other's face, never getting a chance to do things on their own. She granted his request for space as she struggled to understand him. Within three months, they were so

> It's very easy for space to turn into distance and distance to turn into darkness.

160

emotionally separated, they could barely even say good morning to each other. You see, sometimes a partner's request for space leads to an emotionally long-distance relationship. It's very easy for space to turn into distance and distance to turn into darkness, and before you know it, you're emotionally too far apart to even see one another.

Gently, I helped this woman look at her *attitude* about the situation and empowered her to encourage her husband, who was obviously hurting as well. This led them to feel their love's heart-beat again – slowly at first and then eventually at a normal pace. Jane learned new things about Mark. For instance, the reason he wanted space was because, when he was young, he'd always run to his bedroom when his parents argued. When they had a spat, all he knew how to do was ask to leave the room and distance himself from the situation. This gave him a false sense of freedom or independence that he had been trying to reconstruct in his marriage. Mark discovered that he could learn new ways to be free and be close to Jane at the same time. That it didn't have to be an either/or, but could rather be a both/and – a "win-win" situation.

Jane identified very well with how love had stopped flowing through her heart and what happened in her life that affected her ability to regenerate the love she and her husband once had. But with her change in attitude, they now shared some of the most intimate moments of forgiveness that marriage can ever bring to a couple. Broken hearts need help and when they find it, they un-break themselves in remarkable ways, forcing love to live again.

It's very difficult to hide your attitude. Attitudes seep out in the way you look at people, the way you walk and talk, the way you comb your hair, the clothes you choose to wear, and many other things. It's obvious to everyone how people with blatant attitudes feel and what they think about themselves and others. Hiding an attitude is very difficult even temporarily; in the long run, it's impossible. You have probably heard this before: "God, can she please lose the attitude!" It doesn't mean put it in your pocket or your purse – it really means to start all over again. Rewind! Backup! Put on the breaks! Your attitude has gotten in the way of your healthy relationships.

HOW TO CHANGE YOUR ATTITUDE

Since attitudes are a collection of information, thoughts and feelings, you have to address each of these determining factors in order to change or modify your attitude. Changing only how you feel about something does not change your attitude. You have to address the information you have and where you got it from. You have to begin to create new thoughts around the information, build a new interpretation of it and finally allow these new thoughts to influence how you feel about the situation.

A changed attitude will lead to changed actions. When you change your attitude, changed actions will follow automatically. If you have gotten mad at yourself for letting things happen

> A changed attitude will lead to changed actions.

in the past, change that attitude, and you'll change your life.

Here's how to go about changing your attitude:

1. First you have to recognize the attitude.

2. Identify where you learned it. What did those experiences teach you to believe?

3. Begin reinterpreting the information by asking yourself what needs to be changed.

4. Begin to engage in new and healthy relationships. Attitudes are shaped by interaction, so they are also changed through interaction.

5. Practice your new attitude in public. It doesn't help practicing in the mirror. Attitude change is a public issue.

EXERCISES

Forgiveness Phase IV – Revealing
Assignment 1:

Here is a list of questions that can help you think through times you may have needed forgiveness. As you answer these questions, think about whether or not those incidents have been resolved and what you did to seek out forgiveness.

1. What incident do you remember that made someone angry with you?

2. Have you ever been dishonest with anyone? If so, tell what happened.

3. Write about an incident (something that was your fault) that embarrassed you or made you feel shame?

Forgiveness Phase IV – Revealing
Assignment 2:

There are so many things that are different between you and your offender. Write the top five differences between you and the person who broke your heart.

	ME	MY OFFENDER
1.	_____	_____
2.	_____	_____
3.	_____	_____
4.	_____	_____
5.	_____	_____

Forgiveness Phase IV – Revealing
Assignment 3:

Answer the questions below:

1. What are two incidents in your life when you needed someone to forgive you for something?

   a. _____

   b. _____

2. For each of these, describe how it felt to need someone to forgive you?

   a. _____

   b. _____

3. How did knowing that you hurt someone affect you?

   a. _____

   b. _____

REFLECTION NOTES:

How would you summarize your thoughts and feelings after a reading and completing the exercises in this section?

Take the time to come home to yourself every day. ~ Robin Casarjean

CHAPTER 11

PHASE V: RECOVERY

NEW MEMORIES/BETTER CHOICES

The **RECOVERY PHASE is the fifth phase of forgiveness**. In this phase, you begin creating action-oriented tasks for yourself that promote the work you did in the previous phases. You've accepted the event in the first phase; you've matched your emotions to the events and the person who broke your heart in Phase II; you've resolved your anger in Phase III; you have observed the model of forgiveness in scripture in the fourth phase and now you are ready to put things into action. There is an old saying in mental health and addiction circles, common to AA groups and treatment environments, that reflects the ongoing need for recovery: "Once an alcoholic, always an alcoholic." Or even more cryptically, "Once you're pickled, you can never go back to being a cucumber!"

This doesn't mean that you must always or inevitably drink, but it does help to create a consciousness of the risk of slipping back into abuse. The stories of addiction can vary from, "I haven't touched drugs or alcohol in over 40 years" to, "I relapsed after 13 years." Regardless of how long they stayed clean or sober before they used again, a relapsing alcoholic still has the awareness that they need to stop using.

I often tell people in recovery that "you don't start *over* again when you relapse; you simply start from here." The same is true with forgiveness. After you have forgiven someone, you may find that there are some things that still don't sit well with you. When you discover them, you will want to take each of them through the phases of forgiveness.

Cora's Story:

My client told me that she had been upset at her mother for years but, when Cora became a Christian, she decided that she would forgive her mother for all the hardship she had caused in her daughter's life. Thirty years later, as she was walking out of her mother's house after a Sunday visit, her mother simply, compassionately touched her forehead as if to say, "Be blessed," and Cora, to her surprise, felt anger boil up inside her.

Although she didn't tell her mother how angry she was, Cora knew something was wrong. "Why did I feel like that and where did that feeling come from?" she asked, going on to say, "I thought I had forgiven her."

Sometimes your emotions have to catch up with you and sometimes unresolved issues come to the surface that you were not even aware of when you initially forgave that person. The Recovery Phase creates an opportunity for you to live consciously and actively pursue forgiveness. It helps you to start from where you are, rather than making you feel you have to start your life all over again. Recovery is also the fifth and final stage of a broken heart.

Of course, when I say "final," I don't mean that you will never have to revisit your healing journey. There will always be things in life that are worthy of your forgiveness. As life goes

> There will always be things in life that are worthy of your forgiveness.

along, you will find that different situations and relationships bring about various opportunities for you to extend the gift of forgiveness to others. Sometimes you'll feel like doing it and other times you may be a bit hesitant. That's why a recovery mindset is the best approach. It will help you to be more aware of the potential you have to fall back into unforgiveness again.

LIVING LIFE ON PURPOSE

I was sitting in the airport one day and noticed a couple in their late teens. They had a son who looked to be about two years old. As I watched the young father chase his son around the airport, laughing and playing as though he himself were a child, I began to think about how his son would one day grow up and be challenged by life's many experiences. I wondered how life had been for the dad. Was *his* father there for him when he was two years old?

The two played innocently, the little boy enjoying being chased by his dad and the dad pretending to be unable to catch him and falling to the floor in laughter. But I thought how, over time, things would begin to change. The young father would grow older and his son would not stay a child forever. In the next 20 or 30 years, the range of things boy experienced would gradually cover that innocent, laughing face with the mask of adulthood.

Have you ever wanted to start over? Have you ever thought to yourself, "I wish you could go back in time" before a particular incident happened? Maybe you've made some mistakes in relationships or business and thought, "God, if I could just go back and ..." The experience giving rise to such wishful thinking can gradually "put a lid" on your expression of the real you. It's never easy to go forward when your life has been covered by so much. You literally have to start digging to find yourself, because each experience in your past has helped to shape your life and the way you think about yourself.

That's why I tell young people to move slowly in relationships and don't have too many too fast. Every relationship helps shape the way you think and live, and the more stable they are, the more stable you will be.

As your broken heart is healed, love will begin to live again. In one aspect, you are learning a new way of loving by setting boundaries that respect and protect you and by letting go of the past. On the other hand, the old you has to catch up with the new you while you are learning to live and love again. When things are hard and resources are limited (and sometimes they will be), you need to hang on to the hope that forgiveness is healing your broken heart (and it is).

I have seen many tremendously gifted people who were just bogged down by a negative view of themselves. One young lady was as beautiful as could be on the outside, but saw herself as being so ugly on the inside. There is something to the saying, "Don't judge a book by its cover." Just because someone looks good on the outside doesn't mean there isn't turmoil on the inside. But the inside is what matters. Love turns to the inside when the honeymoon phase is over in a marriage. The inside is what cries and struggles in secret when you are abused. It's easy to dress up the outside, but the inside is harder to disguise.

Living with unforgiveness halts the possibility of inside transformation and forces you to settle for the fabricated changes on the outside that don't really make a difference. But living with forgiveness opens your heart and expands your soul so that your inner life becomes pure joy. Then your "skin" becomes transparent, letting that inner glow shine through, and there is no need to add fancy trappings. You become a natural "people magnet."

> Living with unforgiveness halts the possibility of inside transformation...

RECREATING MEMORIES

I was driving home from the office one day and heard the song my wife and I danced to at our wedding. That music carried my emotions right back to the moment we danced, almost 17 years before. It's amazing how the body and the brain create memories and marry those memories to emotions. When you hear a song or see a movie and have one of those *déjà vu* feelings – like you've been there before – it's because you have.

Memories are great when they bring you back to good times, but they can be sad and haunting when they bring you back to bad times. Memories of a broken heart can hold you back from your true destination in life and keep you from reaching your full potential. Since there is no way psychologically to stop your brain from remembering unless you have a memory disorder, it's vital that you help your brain remember well, i.e., in a way that promotes your emotional health and wellbeing. Begin to create new memories for yourself and to reframe old experiences so that you remember anew. Since, as you read previously, forgiveness doesn't forget, you have to teach it how to remember well.

All bad experiences have a glimmer of light in them. When that glimmer is discovered, it gives purpose to the darkness of your broken heart. If it seems like your broken heart is full to overflowing with bad memories, this is the time to begin stuffing your memory bank with brand new memories by getting the most out

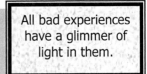

All bad experiences have a glimmer of light in them.

of new and pleasant moments. As you probably know, this memory bank of yours has an unlimited capacity. So it's all a matter of percentages. If you don't add to your positive, hopeful memories on a daily basis, the old negative memories become the majority and rise more often to the surface, plaguing and discouraging you.

Sometimes, in the midst of a pleasant, happy experience, you have to stop and tell yourself that you want to remember it. To help you recall it in the future, match it in that moment with a song or other mnemonic (memory aide). As you constantly create new memories for yourself, you are also creating opportunities for your heart to heal and hope again. Eventually you will find that the emotions of your broken heart experience have been neutralized and you will be able to face them with confidence.

DREAMING AGAIN

When life is hard many people give up on their dreams. As things happen to you in life to break your heart, you may lose sight of your dreams and aspirations. Now that you have worked through the phases of forgiveness, you can to begin to dream again.

At first, all the horrible memories of the events that led to your broken heart will probably flood your mind and make things gloomy and dark. Counter that with the dreams you once had. Pick up right where you left off. Tell yourself what you are going to accomplish and then start taking actions, no matter how small, to do it. This teaches your body that it doesn't control you, but you control it. It can't tell you how to feel and how to live any longer; you are now the boss!

Make sure that you are creating more positive dreams than you have bad memories. That's right – your dreams have to outweigh your memories. Learn to go after more than you went through.

Start being *you* again – embracing all of your experiences and using those experiences to lead you up the path to your future. Since you've just gone through the surgical procedure to have your heart healed – having worked through the phases of forgiveness (I through IV) – now you know that, just because your heart was broken doesn't mean life is over for you. You deserve the best now and the best is waiting to for you to reach out and grab it.

Go out and get it. Be bold and have courage. Defend yourself and your beliefs. Advocate for others who cannot advocate for themselves. Sometimes your dreams come true by helping others accomplish their dreams. Be a dreamer again and set the atmosphere around you to be an environment of positive thinking and ambitious dreamers. Be you, embracing all of your experiences and use your experiences to tread the path to your future.

Here's your dreamer's to-do list:

1. Embrace *all* your experiences;

2. Think positively and create an atmosphere that encourages your dreams;

3. Act on your dreams;

4. Help others achieve their dreams.

GOING FORWARD: MAKING HEALTHY CHOICES

The book of Job is an intense chapter of the Bible, dominated by how this man's faith in God led him to persevere through a treacherous time in his life. But beyond this story of faith is an issue that separates the weak from the strong, the successful from the unsuccessful and the winners from the losers. That is the issue of *integrity*.

Job and Abraham:

Faith is what you believe about God. Integrity is what you do about it. If you really want to experience growth and transformation in your life, you've got to "get" this principle. God honors integrity and that's what separated Job from his friends and even his wife. She was obviously a woman of faith and so was his whole family, but when the rubber met the road (to use a modern metaphor for an old-yet-timeless story), her decision was different than his. As a matter of fact, Job's wife asked him, "Are you still holding on to your integrity? Curse God and die!" (*Job 2:9*) She didn't say, "holding on to your *faith*," but rather "your *integrity*." Many have alleged that she didn't have as much faith as Job, but her faith is not mentioned in scripture. What is revealed is the difference in their integrity. Integrity is about that moment of decision making – that split window of choice, where God graces you with the opportunity to decide what you are going to do. It shows up in your private life and it also visits your public life. Integrity is the thing that brings you to perfect faith by

> Faith is what you believe about God. Integrity is what you do about it.

practicing in your daily life a decision method that honors God and gives direction to the vision God has given you.

Abraham is considered the father of faith, but his momentous decision also reflected his integrity. God again brought about an opportunity to respond with integrity by asking Abraham to sacrifice his son Isaac.

The choices you make in life are assisted by the Life Filtering Chamber of your heart – the last of the four chambers, where the facts, your emotions and your attitudes are all run through a sieve that sorts out joy from sorrow and hope from fear, allowing you to make choices with discernment. Not all choices lead to the same end, but good choices obviously will produce much better results than bad ones. Begin making the kind of choices that speak of *your* integrity. I would hire a person with integrity before I hired the smartest or most experienced person for a job, because in the end only the one who has integrity will also bring total discipline and respect to the position.

> Not all choices lead to the same end, but good choices will produce much better results than bad ones

EXERCISES

Forgiveness Phase V – Recovery
Assignment 1:

Make a list below of your old dreams and how a broken heart impacted those dreams. Then write what you learned in the summary below. Use as much space as you need (it's o.k. to color outside the lines).

    a. **Old dream**

    b. **Events that impacted it**

1. a. _____

   b. _____

2. a. _____

   b. _____

3. a. _____

   b. _____

Write a summary about what insights you gained from seeing how your broken heart impacted your dreams.

Forgiveness Phase V – Recovery
Assignment 2:

Sometimes memories help us determine what we need to be dreaming of to make things better for ourselves. Bad memories can prompt you to help others keep from experiencing what you experienced. Memories of feeling unappreciated can help you dream of appreciating yourself and placing yourself in relationships where you are appreciated. In the space below, write down old memories and match them with new dreams.

    a. **Bad memory**

    b. **New dream**

1. a. _____

    b. _____

2. a. _____

    b. _____

3. a. _____

    b. _____

Forgiveness Phase V – Recovery
Assignment 3:

What healthy choices do you need to make in your life?
There may be some things you need to change right now
and others that you need to work towards. Write them
down in the space below.

1. _____

2. _____

3. _____

4. _____

5. _____

Forgiveness Phase V – Recovery
Assignment 4:

Write a brief letter to your own heart telling it how you feel about it and what your plans are for it in the future.

Forgiveness is the fragrance that the violet sheds on the heel that has crushed it. ~ Mark Twain

CHAPTER 12

TWO OUTPATIENT CHECKUPS

OK, you made it through your open-heart surgery, you're out of the recovery room and back home. Now you only have two outpatient appointments left. During these appointments, we will address two final issues related to forgiveness. The first is reconciliation and the second is how you can know you have truly forgiven someone. As the doctor would say, "Let's make sure you keep these appointments."

APPOINTMENT 1: ON RECONCILIATION

I know the big question in relationships is most often whether or not forgiveness should lead to reconciliation between the people involved. As important as I think the question is, I want to approach reconciliation from the perspective of how forgiveness works.

As I have discussed throughout the book, forgiveness is the scalpel we use to perform emergency surgery on the broken heart. Forgiveness is about healing the deep wounds of the heart that were produced by an offense and is intended to help the person whose heart is broken.

Therefore, it isn't necessary for both people to be involved in the process. It is obviously more beneficial for the person who has been hurt when an offender does request forgiveness, but it is not necessary.

During my counseling career, there have been many people who decided, for the sake of closure, to visit the gravesite of an offender who had passed away, to let them know that they were forgiven for what they did. Empty chairs have been used in counseling sessions to role-play the presence of the offender as well.

What role does reconciliation play in forgiveness? First, let me say that reconciliation is the very substance of forgiveness. Forgiveness serves to reconcile the internal elements of pain and put things back together so the mind can build a fresh perspective of it all. Forgiveness carefully begins to reconnect emotional experiences as it heals the hurts and pains of those bad experiences. When working with victims, we have to start from inside the heart and then make decisions for the outside that will ensure that the heart is safeguarded. So reconciliation needs to occur in a safe environment and be appropriate for the people involved.

> Forgiveness serves to ... put things back together.

Katrina's Story:

Katrina was raped by a family friend when she was very young. She was too afraid to tell anyone because she thought people would blame her and be upset with her. The abuser had also threatened to hurt another family member if she ever told, so the abuse went on for years, beginning at age seven. Katrina confided that, after a while, her brain was able to turn off the pain and "almost escape to another place" while the abuse occurred. She said that her brain and body became so disconnected that she eventually stopped thinking about her body at all and started making really bad decisions concerning it. She concluded that life was lonely, and she could feel herself getting "sicker" as she silently cried out for help.

Katrina's cry was one that nobody could hear but herself until she got married and began to have problems in her sexual relationship with her husband. She always felt embarrassed and uncomfortable with sex. She tried her best to connect with her husband, but the more she tried the harder things got for her. Eventually Katrina came to therapy and began to work through the issues related to her past abuse.

Where many counselors would have treated her sexual dysfunction, I decided to examine Katrina's history and help her work on forgiving her abuser. As she began to go through the phases of forgiveness, she discovered that she was not only disconnected from her husband, but also separated within herself. She was detached from her own body. The abused body parts, which her young brain had decided were dirty and humiliating, disconnected themselves as though they did not belong to her anymore. That's how she was able to be in so many promiscuous relationships during adolescence, telling herself, "It's just sex." She never made the connection between sex and her body.

Katrina's therapeutic work was to reconnect those parts of her body and learn to love her whole self again. Retraining her brain to restore hope to her body and helping herself to understand that they were clean – that she was not dirty and unworthy of a healthy relationship based on love – was her goal. She wanted to believe that someone – especially her husband – could love the person she was now and be able to use all she had to offer. Then she began to take a close look at the redemptive acts of God as He forgave her of all her sins. She wept and said, "If He did that for me, I know I can forgive."

Katrina allowed the Spirit of God to humble her; instead of letting her brain try to protect her by separating her experiences from her feelings, she now asked God to protect her. And God began to bring things back together for her. She learned that her body was hers, regardless of any of the misfortunes it had suffered, and that it was worthy of respect and honor. As she continued to work through the phases of forgiveness, her marriage began to get better as well. She learned that forgiveness, at its core, brings things together.

We may well ask whether or not we should always reconcile with the perpetrator when we forgive. In my opinion, even though the essence of forgiveness is internal reconciliation, it may not and should not always lead to external reconciliation. External reconciliation needs to be processed by the two people involved. Sometimes it is unsafe to reconcile and sometimes it is unreasonable and even inappropriate. You have to weigh your options when considering reconciling to an offender.

But, if you do the internal work, you'll be better prepared to make a decision about reconciling. Remember, just because people get back together doesn't mean they've forgiven and just because people have forgiven doesn't mean they should get back together. The two are far from being synonymous. Just as forgiving is not forgetting, forgetting is not forgiving.

APPOINTMENT 2: 43 WAYS TO KNOW YOU HAVE FORGIVEN

The big question for those who try to live a life of forgiveness is, "how do I know I've forgiven someone?" As you have read in previous chapters, many people who thought they had forgiven someone simply by saying the words later found out that they had not resolved and reconciled the issues of their heart. Therefore, forgiveness had not occurred.

I thought that it would be great to close our book with some general benefits of forgiveness that may serve as signs that you have truly forgiven someone. This is not intended to be the end-all of lists of the positive things you may notice once you've started genuinely forgiving, but I think it will help you assess whether you have at least made some advances in your skills as a forgiving person. And I am confident that, by the time you've gotten this far, checking off those benefits you have gained will reassure you that you have indeed made wonderful progress.

1. You are more accepting of your past failures and misfortunes in general.

2. You have an inner peace about your offender and the events surrounding the incident(s).

3. You have increased self-value and see yourself as being an important contributor to society.

4. You are not ashamed or embarrassed about who you are and you are proud of yourself.

5. You have more improved and healthy relationships in your life than you have unhealthy ones.

6. You are joyful and motivated more than you are depressed and anxious.

7. You are less fearful and more in control of your decisions.

8. You make healthy choices that are based on information, not anger, guilt and frustration.

9. You are able to use your offender's name without feeling irritated or uncomfortable.

10. You have full control of your emotions, rather than their having control over you.

11. You don't feel "stuck" in life or as if your life is going in circles.

12. You don't try to prove to others that you are strong or that you survived.

13. You are more content in life and life's situations.

14. You have a reliance on God to protect, guide and strengthen you.

15. You are more appreciative of God's love for you.

16. You do not feel guilty all the time.

17. You are not afraid to talk about the incident that broke your heart.

18. You live with fewer regrets.

19. You are no longer angry towards your offender and less angry in general.

20. You get mad much more slowly than you used to and when you do get mad you're able to control it.

21. You feel inspired by your life and experiences.

22. You are able to think about the past and have no feelings of defeat, depression, anxiety or anger around it.

23. You feel good when you hear good things about your offender.

24. You don't feel like you got the "short end of the stick" anymore.

25. You are not jealous of what others have and don't feel like you have to compete with everybody.

26. You have a genuine inclination to want to see others do better than you and help them if you can.

27. You are less stressful in general and strive to take good care of yourself.

28. You are increasingly kind and generous towards others.

29. You have a positive view about people who remind you of your offender or who have similar characteristics.

30. You handle change more effectively than you used to.

31. You are self-determined and self-motivated.

32. You are able to set healthy boundaries for yourself and others in your life.

33. You are more trusting of others and less suspicious that people are "out to hurt you" or that a certain gender (male/female) is "no good."

34. You are able to handle conflict in a healthy and appropriate way.

35. You make more rational than irrational decisions.

36. You are more positive than you are negative.

37. You enjoy being around people who are more accomplished than you.

38. You like learning from others.

39. You are able to receive gifts and help without feeling like you shouldn't or that you don't deserve it.

40. You don't take everything personally and are able to separate your personal life from your business life.

41. You don't live to make up for your losses, but you try to get the most out of the moments you have.

42. You are less critical of other people and situations.

43. You are open to constructive criticism and feedback from others concerning your weaknesses.

Remember, there could be many more statements of positive change on this list. Still, it does illustrate how forgiveness has the potential to change your life forever.

Forgiveness is the best medicine for the soul and it costs nothing. It is one of the most powerful human experiences you will ever know and, when you utilize it in your life, it is sure to bring peace to your broken heart.

A loving heart is the truest wisdom. ~ Charles Dickens

CONCLUSION

YOUR NEW HEART

I hope this book has been a blessing to your life. You have come out of surgery and God has healed your broken heart, so now live your life on purpose. Your prognosis looks good provided you continue to walk by faith and trust God in all things.

There is a marvelous world just outside the doors of the waiting room of your life. Open them wide, breathe in the fresh air and walk through them and out into the sunshine with radiant confidence and a glowing smile, knowing that your life will never be the same from now on – it's only going to get better.

May the rest of your life be the best of your life.

Sincerely,

Leroy Scott

Professional Christian Counselor

CONTACT INFORMATION

Leroy Scott Ministries
5635 Main Street / Suite A / #184
Zachary, LA 70791
(407) 622-6121
www.leroyscott.com
email: leroyscott@leroyscott.com

OTHER PRODUCTS

Creating Possibilities in Marriage

ISBN: 9781615794362

Copyright: 2009

Price: $ 9.99

Love Notes:
28 Ways to Deepen Your Love Life

ISBN: 978-0-615-78278-2

Copyright: 2013

Price: $23.99

To order visit
www.leroyscott.com